"Lisa's poems are captivating to the heart. Her words are potent, powerful, and penetrating. Whether a word that uplifts, a phrase that creates peace, or a reminder of Truth....Lisa Neu's poems impact readers and are easy to understand, connect with, and continue to resonate in the heart long after having been read."

Amie Gamboian—National Mary Kay Director,
Mentor, Business Coach, and Speaker

"Lisa Neu's inspirational poetry touches my soul in a deeply intimate way. And yet it is universal in it's treatment of feelings that all of us experience. I would recommend this book to anyone who wish to deepen their relationship with Christ."

Mary Bernier—Owner of Inspired Giving:
Changing the World through Philanthropy

"The inspiration of Lisa's poems soothe my heart, my mind, my soul.... creates memories, and present and future goals, as I read her enlightening words that I apply to my life daily."

John Lee Hoich—Entrepreneur and Author of
"From the Ground Up"

The FINGERS *of* GOD

LISA MICHELE NEU

WESTBOW
PRESS®
A DIVISION OF THOMAS NELSON
& ZONDERVAN

WestBow Press books may be ordered through booksellers or by contacting:

WestBow Press
A Division of Thomas Nelson & Zondervan
1663 Liberty Drive
Bloomington, IN 47403
www.westbowpress.com
1 (866) 928-1240

Because of the dynamic nature of the Internet, any web addresses or links contained in this book may have changed since publication and may no longer be valid. The views expressed in this work are solely those of the author and do not necessarily reflect the views of the publisher, and the publisher hereby disclaims any responsibility for them.

NIV
Scripture quotations marked NIV are taken from the Holy Bible, New International Version®. NIV®. Copyright © 1973, 1978, 1984 by International Bible Society. Used by permission of Zondervan. All rights reserved. [Biblica]

Any people depicted in stock imagery provided by Thinkstock are models, and such images are being used for illustrative purposes only. Certain stock imagery © Thinkstock.

ISBN: 978-1-9736-0390-0 (sc)
ISBN: 978-1-9736-0391-7 (hc)
ISBN: 978-1-9736-0389-4 (e)

Library of Congress Control Number: 2017915282

Print information available on the last page.

WestBow Press rev. date: 01/30/2018

I would like to dedicate this book to my late mother,
Oneta Lavonne Riggs,
who taught me the true beauty of Christian poetry.

Also dedicated to my two beautiful daughters,
Michaela and Jennifer,
who have grown up to be strong, intelligent, Christian women,
who inspire me every day.
May God bless you both always!

CONTENTS

ACKNOWLEDGMENTS

Special thanks to my dear friend, Susan,
who proofed and edited the final manuscript.
This was so very much appreciated!

Also, special thanks to WestBow Press
for their time and patience,
and for pulling this book together in such a beautiful way.

THE FINGERS OF GOD

The Fingers of God reached down today,
bursting forth through a cloud-filled sky.
The brilliant rays of God's mighty hand
reaching down for you and I.

Like a rainbow that captivates and holds
a beauty beyond compare,
in awestruck wonder it held for me
a vision both amazing and rare.

It's as if God is saying, "I'm here for you.
Take My hand and don't let go.
Sense My assurance, mercy, and grace;
no greater love you'll ever know."

The next time you see the Fingers of God,
reaching down from Heaven above,
know that in this most marvelous way,
God is showing His Heaven-sent love.

The heavens declare the glory of God;
the skies proclaim the work of his hands.
Psalm 19:1

A DROP IN THE BUCKET

"A drop in the bucket." What does this mean?
Is it a low servant who works for a king?

Is it one snowflake in a wintry storm?
Is it a kernel in a field of corn?

Is it a petal in a garden of flowers?
Is it a raindrop in gentle spring showers?

Is it a stream that flows to the ocean?
Is it one muscle of a body in motion?

Is it one tear in the throes of deep sorrow?
Is it one faith in the hopes of tomorrow?

Is it one second in the vastness of time?
Is it one mountain in our path we must climb?

Is it one thought in the lifetime of knowledge?
Is it the wisdom of one scholar in college?

Is it one memory in the union of love?
Is it one prayer to our Father above?

But know in all of the things God has taught,
truly a "drop in the bucket" we're not.

For all of life's "drops" are part of a whole,
and each has its purpose and each has a role.

And we know that in all things God works for the good
of those who love him, who have been called according to his purpose.
Romans 8:28

A MOMENT'S GRACE

A moment's grace is all I need
when I have gone astray.
I know, dear Lord, your grace is there
as I walk life's path each day.

A moment's grace I do desire
when redemption is what I need.
What mighty grace, dear Lord, you give
when forgiveness is what I plead.

A moment's grace is always there,
unworthy though I may be.
I am, dear Lord, most thankful that
your grace pours down on me.

A moment's grace is all it took
when you died upon the cross.
You looked upon the sins of man
and said "it's worth the cost."

A moment's grace is amazing, and
I thank you, Lord, for same;
for granting peace and mercy when
I call upon your name.

A moment's grace, what peace I know,
when striving to do your will;
for I know, dear Lord, each time I fail
your grace remains there still!

For it is by grace you have been saved, through faith -
and this not from yourselves, it is the gift of God -
not by works, so that no one can boast.
Ephesians 2:8-9

A NEW NORMAL

Life happens. There are changes.
New routines up ahead.
The old is out, part of the past.
A new normal is here instead.

It could be from an awakening;
a spiritual decision made.
A lifestyle change renewal.
The old normal now will fade.

It could be from the passing
of a dear beloved one.
The loss means more than one can know.
A new normal has begun.

It may be from health issues,
yours or someone whom you know.
Your life may change forever.
A new normal now will show.

It could be a career change
or retirement now your path.
Don't fret or let change scare you.
A new normal is what you have.

Change may not be sought or wanted;
many stresses may abound.
But know in all life's changes
a new normal will be found.

See, the former things have taken place,
and new things I declare ...
Isaiah 42:9

A SHIPWRECKED FAITH

A shipwrecked faith is still a faith
though you've crashed upon life's shore.
You may have hit rock bottom
and feel you can sail no more.

But God has other plans for you,
perhaps now's the time to fly.
Time to put away those sails,
and give your "wings" a try.

You may feel that there's no making right
all the wrongs that you have done.
But God, in His deep love for us,
sent His one and only Son.

To help us when we've shipwrecked
and when we're calling out to Him;
when our faith has failed and our soul is weak,
and we're burdened by our sin.

Perhaps it's time to spread your wings;
a time that you just know
to place your faith and trust in God.
A time to just let go.

So, crawl out of that shipwreck,
walk away from your past sin,
and know that through this wreckage
new life will now begin.

… holding on to faith and a good conscience.
Some have rejected these and so have shipwrecked their faith.
1 Timothy 1:19

A SONG

I have a song within my heart
that's playing soft and low;
a constant humming deep within
of praise both sweet and slow.

I'm sure it's the Holy Spirit
who resides within my heart;
I feel its mighty power,
in which the music plays a part.

It surely is the Christian joy,
knowing salvation's here to stay;
the music drifts throughout my being
and will never go away.

So, let the beat within your soul
spring forth from rivers deep,
like a fountain ever flowing with
a song you'll always keep.

The Lord is my strength and my shield;
my heart trusts in him, and I am helped.
My heart leaps for joy and I will give him thanks in song."
Psalm 28:7

A STILL SMALL VOICE

A still small voice is calling
in the regions of your mind;
it is giving you direction,
and true wisdom there you'll find.

God speaks through that still small voice
of the things that you should hear,
giving guidance and instruction
and direction, sure and clear.

God speaks through His creation,
through the prophets and Holy Word.
He speaks to our hearts with conviction
in hopes His still, small voice is heard.

We'll know that when we hear it,
the Holy Spirit does abound.
We can trust in the guidance whispered,
where unending love is found.

For God is speaking to us
in that quiet, still, small voice.
And whether or not we heed it
is our own-decided choice.

But the wisdom gained by listening
is worth far more than gold.
So, listen for that voice,
and be guided by what you're told.

*The Lord said, "Go out and stand on the mountain in the presence of the Lord,
for the Lord is about to pass by." Then a great and powerful wind tore the
mountains apart and shattered the rocks before the Lord, but the Lord was
not in the wind. After the wind there was an earthquake, but the Lord was not
in the earthquake. After the earthquake came a fire, but the Lord was not in the fire.
And after the fire came a gentle whisper.*
1 Kings 19:11-12

A STRONGER FLAME

Help me be a stronger flame, Lord, when tested by life's wind.
Fan this flame to a greater blaze, Lord,
revealing faith and discipline.

Help me be a strong foundation, standing firm when called upon.
Not to crumble under life's burdens,
holding fast when hope is gone.

Help me be a warm, safe shelter; an umbrella for those in need.
They can surely feel Thy presence
in this haven from sin and greed.

Help me be a song for singing, praising God our Father above.
Thanking Him for sending Jesus,
our sweet Savior, Lord of love.

Help me be the eyes so daring for the many who cannot see
that Christ's love was sealed and binding
when sacrificed upon the tree.

Help me be the prayer for sinners when their words cannot express
their need to say, "I'm sorry,"
and the faults they must confess.

Help me blow the trumpet, Father, beat the drum for all to hear.
Proclaiming from the rooftops
of salvation, free and dear.

Help me be the strong flame, Father, burning brighter each passing day,
leading many to Thy throne, Lord;
the flame to ever guide their way.

"In the same way, let your light shine before men,
that they may see your good deeds and praise your Father in heaven.
Matthew 5:16

A VOICE IN THE DESERT

Let us be like John the Baptist,
the voice of one, extolling all
to make straight the way for our Lord Jesus;
turn to Him and accept His call.

Be baptized and accept a gift given freely;
though ages pass, things remain the same.
Like John, we are unworthy to untie His sandals;
even so, Christ willingly gave up all and came.

Knowing death was at the end of His journey,
His mission with John was filled full of love.
The Holy Spirit would come straight down from heaven
and settle on Him in the form of a dove.

John proclaimed Christ would be guide and teacher,
leading the way to Heaven's grand gate.
He cried out from the desert to all who would listen,
"Believe now and repent ... before it's too late!"

Yes, Jesus is our dear Lord and Savior;
John loudly proclaimed this from both sea and land
that Christ would baptize with the mighty Holy Spirit
and testified Jesus was the great "Son of Man."

So be like John, though we be unworthy,
calling out from the desert to all who will hear
that Jesus has left us the dear Holy Spirit
and, so equipped, share salvation is near!

The next day John saw Jesus coming toward him and said,
"Look, the Lamb of God, who takes away the sin of the world!"
John 1:29

A VOICE IN THE NIGHT

A Voice in the night whispers softly,
"What have you done today?
Have you done the deeds I've asked of you?
For whom did you earnestly pray?"

A Voice in the night whispers softly,
"Did you care for the sick and the poor?
Did you quietly caress a tired brow?
Did you soothe the weak and the sore?"

A Voice in the night whispers softly,
"Was there a lost soul to be found?
Did you proclaim the Word of God?
Did you tell how God's saints will be crowned?"

A Voice in the night whispers softly,
"What have you done today?"
Reflect on the deeds that were left undone,
and remember to earnestly pray.

And let us consider how we may spur one another on
toward love and good deeds.
Hebrews 10:24

A WHOLE NEW "LIGHTER" DAY

Are you dragging the past around with you
like a heavy ball and chain
that pulls and strains behind you
causing heartache and deep pain?

Do you let yesterday's worries
get in the way of today?
Do you hang on to hurt feelings
of what others do and say?

Are you crippling your emotions
by never letting go
of the heavy baggage of life's burdens
with its weight that you must tow?

It's time to ditch the ball and chain.
Time to lighten life's heavy load.
Time to look at a brighter tomorrow.
Travel lighter on life's road.

Do not drag the past around with you.
Look forward to today.
And all the "good" God offers
will surely come your way.

When others try to weigh you down
with their burdens on display,
remember you're taking a different path
to a whole new "lighter" day!

"Therefore, I tell you, do not worry about your life …
Who of you by worrying can add a single hour to his life?"
Matthew 6:25-27

ACTIONS SPEAK LOUDER

Jesus came to Earth to show us how to live our lives on Earth;
He did this so remarkably
in his arrival through sacred birth.

The Bible, through the ages, tells us what we need to know,
but God knew it'd be more fitting
for Christ to come to Earth to "show".

Jesus didn't just say, "Be humble." He humbled Himself instead;
He did so with humility
in the modest life He led.

He didn't just say, "Forgive others for all the wrongs that come your way."
He exemplified true forgiveness
by hanging on the cross that day.

Telling us about forgiveness can help us understand,
but showing is more effective,
hence the nails through feet and hands.

Christ came as the perfect example of how we daily ought to live.
His actions spoke much louder
than any words could ever give.

"I have set you an example
that you should do as I have done for you."
John 13:15

AGING

I've earned every line upon my face;
every gray hair on my head;
I pray each one's reflective
of the things I've done and said.

I'll wear both proudly in this life,
like a trophy won from a race;
knowing I've done the best I could
through God's love and mighty grace.

I know before this life does end
I'll earn many more, I'm sure.
I may grow weak and my body frail,
but with God's strength I will endure.

I'll be thankful for all God has blessed me with,
especially the friends I've known,
for all I've experienced in this life
and the "seeds of faith" I've sown.

And when it's time to say goodbye
to this life that I have lived,
I hope I've helped all that I could
and gave all I could give.

I only pray that God's beauty there
is reflective to the end;
and of all the wrinkles and grays I've gained,
each one I'll proudly defend!

Even when I am old and gray, do not forsake me, O God,
Till I declare your power to the next generation,
Your might to all who are to come.
Psalm 71:18

ANSWERED PRAYER

We don't always get what we want in life,
but God is always there.
Just because we've asked, we may not receive,
but it still is answered prayer.

We often think because we have prayed
the answer will surely be "yes."
But if our request does not come right away,
then the answer's been delayed, we guess.

But God, in His Fatherly wisdom, knows
all about us and our future can see.
And perhaps His response is a resounding, "no."
For what we've asked for is not to be.

So, trust that God has complete control.
He surely knows what's best to do.
And trust the results of your fervent prayer
is the answer He wants for you!

For the eyes of the Lord are on the righteous
and his ears are attentive to their prayer ...
1 Peter 3:12

AS WE LINGER AT THE THRESHOLD

Why do we wait to say the heartfelt things
just before we say goodbye,
expressing the thoughts that were left unsaid
and our silence did not imply?

Why did we wait to say all these things
while lingering at the door,
though earlier talking, though not saying much,
while together the hours before?

As we gather now at the doorway,
words expressed were not the plan,
but we linger there before parting
squeezing in all the words we can.

We want to express the love we feel
before the parting of our ways,
for we know not what the future holds,
nor the number of our days.

We want our loved ones to know we care
before traveling on down the road.
So, we linger at the threshold
saying the things that must be told.

As we linger one more moment,
with love reflected in our face,
we'll share a kiss or say a prayer
as we snatch one last embrace.

And if our words at the doorway
do not convey the love we feel,
it's surely expressed in our actions,
that in our lingering we reveal.

Pleasant words are a honeycomb,
sweet to the soul and healing to the bones.
Proverbs 16:24

AT HIS FEET

At His feet, I lay my load;
no better place for same.
I've been lugging it around too long;
weighing heavy on my frame.

At His feet, I fall on my knees;
I bow my head to pray.
While kneeling there, I see the scars
that nails had pierced one day.

At His feet, I pour out my tears;
He surely feels them on His toes,
where each one falls as it trickles down
while sharing my fears and woes.

At His feet, I talk with Him,
expressing my hopes and dreams,
revealing the plans and goals I make.
He understands it seems.

At His feet, He lifts me up
though I've often been there before,
finding relief from the heavy loads
that have left me tired and sore.

At His feet, I find the rest
and the blessed peace I seek.
I'll always know I'm welcome there,
no matter how weary and weak.

At His feet, I'll worship Him,
giving Him the glory and praise,
knowing I'll find His mercy and grace,
both now and through all my days.

"Come to me, all you who are weary and burdened,
and I will give you rest."
Matthew 11:28

AT THE END OF THE RAINBOW

While looking at the fork in the road,
deciding which way to go,
did I miss the sun's rays breaking through the clouds
and the sky's panoramic show?

While looking at the hole in the ground,
did I miss the rainbow above,
displaying its brilliant colors
reflecting God's promise and love?

While studying the crack in the sidewalk,
did I miss the setting sun's gleam,
that in its descending glory
streaked the sky in brilliant beam?

While looking down at my dusty shoes,
did I miss the shooting star
that streaked across the twilight sky
and was seen both near and far?

Remember while walking through this life
and the distractions that it can hold,
keep your head held high and your eyes on Christ,
then you won't miss God's "pot of gold!"

Let us fix our eyes on Jesus,
the author and perfecter of our faith....
Hebrews 12:2

BE CHEERFUL

When the winter snows are settling
on the hills outside your door
in the quietness of the morning
before your feet should touch the floor,
remember to whisper thankfulness
to our precious Lord above
for all that life may hold for you
and for His mighty love.

We are told to think the good thoughts.
Don't let Satan bring you down
with worries, frets, and anxieties;
your face reflecting frowns.
Smile away your many troubles.
Be cheerful for what comes your way.
And let God direct your spirit
in the things you think and say.

Finally, brothers, whatever is true, whatever is noble,
whatever is right, whatever is pure, whatever is lovely,
whatever is admirable - if anything is excellent or praiseworthy -
think about such things.
Philippians 4:8

BE THANKFUL

Now is the time to be thankful
for all that God has done,
and to reflect upon His blessings,
counting each and every one.

Think about each blessing
that God has sent your way.
Thank Him for those blessings
that He gives to you each day.

Don't take God's gifts for granted,
don't push each one aside;
but reflect upon His goodness;
let Him always be your guide.

For great is our mighty Father;
most worthy of our praise.
His greatness none can fathom.
We must thank Him all our days.

God is standing near to bless you.
He has gifts for you in store.
He says, "Ask and I'll give to you."
He will give you much and more.

So, say a prayer of thankfulness,
always knowing God is near,
and think upon God's blessings,
each one sanctioned with love sincere.

Great is the Lord and most worthy of praise;
His greatness no one can fathom.
Psalms 145:3

BELIEVE IN ME

Believe in Me, yes, trust in Me;
I've walked this way before.
I've been there, done that, felt the pain
of every slammed and locked-tight door.

Believe in Me when times are tough,
when you feel you can't go on;
when you've ran life's race and feel you've lost,
when you feel all hope is gone.

Believe in Me when you feel alone,
when no one seems to care.
Please know I'm always by your side,
you are blessed beyond compare.

Believe in Me when you're stretched too far;
when you're weary from life's load.
I'll carry that heavy burden for you
on every rough and uphill road.

Believe in Me when life's going great.
Don't forget me when times are good.
Remember the times I've held you close
when you doubted that I would.

Believe in Me, yes, trust in Me;
I've given My all to you.
I came to Earth to point the way
on a path that's walked by few.

"Do not let your hearts be troubled.
Trust in God; trust also in me."
John 14:1

BEYOND DEATH'S SHADOW

The loss of love and life and laughter
when a loved one passes on
can seem more than one can handle now the light of life seems gone.

But God knows that in this deep-felt loss
there is a heavenly plan,
and knows the path you now must follow; has known since time began.

We know not when our time will come;
know not the time or place.
That's why we place our heart and soul within God's heavenly grace.

Certain moments in our lives will happen
that are out of our control;
perhaps beyond our comprehension, certain things we cannot know.

Death to us seems so final,
much more than we can bear;
but if we look beyond death's shadow, we will see God's purpose there.

So, hold your head up higher,
and pray for God to help you through
the loss of a dear loved one; revealing all you now must do.

Look at death as another chapter
to a life God has ordained,
and know that now your loved one received God's treasures to be claimed.

God's plan for love and life and laughter
does not end for you this day.
You're now going a new direction, trust God's plan along the way!

Even though I walk through the valley of the shadow of death,
I will fear no evil, for you are with me;
your rod and your staff, they comfort me.
Psalm 23:4

BLESS ME, LORD

Bless me, Lord, with flowing tears that will cleanse my eyes to see
the painful plight of my fellow man, whatever their burdens be.

Bless me, Lord, with an aching heart so I'll feel another's grief
when they're feeling lost and all alone, help me share with them belief.

Bless me, Lord, with tired feet as I walk in another's shoes,
so I'll understand each burden and trial on the path that they did choose.

Bless me, Lord, with a weary soul that I'll feel another's despair,
that I'll place myself within their path, and they'll know I truly care.

Bless me, Lord, with a listening ear being attentive to those in need.
Help me speak less and listen more to the things of which they plead.

Bless me, Lord, with abundant wealth and a desire to give my all
toward each and every need I see … all needs, both great and small.

Bless me, Lord, with your mercy and grace, and a strength beyond my own.
Let my sole purpose in this life be leading others to your throne!

*"Blessed are those who hunger and thirst for righteousness,
for they will be filled."*
Matthew 5:6

BLESSED BY THE BEST

It's wonderful to know you're in a good place
and to feel completely satisfied
in having the knowledge you've truly been blessed
with God's gifts to you multiplied.

You'll walk daily the path He's pointing you to,
and you'll know you are going the right way.
You'll feel it within the depth of your soul
and know He walks with you each day.

You'll be a success in all that you do,
and you'll sense the presence of His love.
You'll know in the failures and victories of life
that your strength comes from God above.

And when you're scared and doubts filter in,
stand up tall, put a smile on your face;
square up your shoulders, hold your head high,
and you'll always be a winner in life's race.

You must always seek His grace and His plan,
and realize in all that you do;
that if you retain a servant-like heart,
God will always be there for you.

Know that when you strive for His will,
you'll daily continue to be blessed.
God will see you through every trial and triumph,
and you'll know you are blessed by the best!

"For I know the plans I have for you," declares the Lord,
"plans to proper you and not to harm you,
plans to give you hope and a future."
Jeremiah 29:11

BLESSINGS IN DISGUISE

Why do we hold back teardrops
when there's heartache and much pain,
for there is healing in those teardrops like the cleansing drops of rain?

Why do our many trials
reflect sadness through our eyes,
when trials make us stronger and are blessings in disguise?

Why does every wrong turn
that we take throughout the day
cause such irritation when God's pointing out the way?

Why does every heartbreak
hurt so much within our soul,
for it's a true-life lesson God wants each of us to know?

Why do all our daily sins
make us feel unworthy and untrue?
We must remember we are human, and Christ died for me and you.

Why do we feel like losers
when we fail in this life's race,
for though we may not measure up, we still receive God's grace?

Though we may shed many teardrops
and there's sadness in our eyes,
we know that each trial and heartache are God's blessings in disguise!

Consider it pure joy, my brothers, whenever you face trials of many kinds,
because you know that the testing of your faith develops perseverance.
James 1:2-3

BLOOM

A flower blooms where it is planted;
nothing seems to hold it back.
It flourishes in its glory and in beauty does not lack.

It reaches for the heavens
while its vibrant colors show;
seeking rain, as well as sunshine, and God's love to help it grow.

From the time the seed is planted
to the time it is in bloom,
it is part of God's creation, supplying Earth with sweet perfume.

We too can bloom where planted,
for God has a special plan;
we are right where He does want us … this was so since time began.

We should not fuss or worry,
letting troubles hold us back,
nor fret about the future or the things that we might lack.

We should trust the plans God has for us,
both in beauty and design;
unique in our creation as we daily thrive and shine.

Always reaching for the heavens
while our vibrant colors show;
reflecting God's created beauty as we flourish, live, and grow.

For God loves all His creation,
so much more He does love man.
He has planted us where He wants us, with a purpose and a plan.

"Who of you by worrying can add a single hour to his life?
And why do you worry about clothes? See how the lilies of the field grow.
They do not labor or spin. Yet I tell you that not even Solomon in all his splendor
was dressed like one of these."
Matthew 6:27-29

Is your name in the Book of Heaven?
Is it written there with flair?
It wasn't from your good works
that God has placed it there.

You cannot work your good deeds
and think that you have won
a special place in Heaven -
That's just not how it is done.

There are many religions abounding;
listen closely to what they teach.
If they ask, "Do you believe in God?"
be careful at what they preach.

Their God may be a false one,
their deed to lead astray;
but you know that through the Bible
there is only one true way.

The way is through Christ Jesus,
who came and died for you.
If others tell you differently,
you know what you must do.

Tell them of the precious Jesus,
who died on Earth for them.
He hung upon the sacred cross
to save, not to condemn.

Your name's in the Book of Heaven.
It is written there with flair.
Because of your belief in Jesus,
God has placed it proudly there.

"… but rejoice that your names are written in heaven."
Luke 10:20

BOUNCE BACK

Did you know that palm trees
bend but do not break?
Like all of God's creations,
special features He did make.

Palm trees are in locations
where hurricane winds may blow;
you won't see them on the mountaintop
surrounded by ice and snow.

You will not find a pine tree
on a deserted tropical isle,
nor flourishing oak or elm trees
growing along the Egyptian Nile.

God knew the perfect environment
for every tree and plant to thrive
and adapts each to their placement
to weather storms and still survive.

If He does this for tree and plant life,
and all creatures on this Earth,
you know He has made each one of us
"perfection" at our birth.

And like the bendable palm trees
in our troubled winds of life,
we will bounce right back to standing
when we're bent by fear and strife.

For God has made us "perfect"
in our unique and special way.
We will flourish like the palm tree
if we'll trust in God each day.

The righteous will flourish like a palm tree ...
Psalm 92:12

BRING IT ON

Bring it on, Lord, bring it on;
I feel I'm ready now.
The rapture can happen anytime soon
though we know not when or how.

But if the rapture should happen today, Lord,
would all whom I know be saved,
or are they still lost in this lonely world,
not knowing the sin you forgave?

People have waited for centuries, Lord,
but your timing we know is best;
we just have to wait and be patient,
for there are others that still may need blessed.

So, bring it on, Lord, bring it on,
but do so in your own time.
Help us lead others to you, Lord,
so our loved ones are not left behind.

*"No one knows about that day or hour, not even the angels in heaven,
nor the Son, but only the Father."*
Matthew 24:36

BROKEN HEARTS

Broken hearts - broken dreams,
broken lives - so it seems.
Feeling abandoned - walking alone,
fears of tomorrow - future unknown.

Searching for answers - denying what's true,
uncertainty come - options are few.
Confusion and anger - frustrations abound,
true peace is sought - not often found.

Crying out to God - seeking answers to prayer,
head bowing, soul searching - knowing He's there.
Holding you closely - carrying you through,
lifting you up - in all that you do.

Broken hearts - broken dreams,
broken lives - so it seems.
Don't feel lost - not walking alone,
no fear of tomorrow - God's presence is known.

For this God is our God for ever and ever;
He will be our guide even to the end.
Psalm 48:14

CAN'T BREATHE

Have you ever had a moment that just takes your breath away?
That pressure deep within your chest
that causes some dismay.

The moment of something beautiful, a stunning sunrise or sunset;
or seeing a family resemblance
in a sibling you've just met.

Perhaps the grand formation of magnificent geese in flight,
or the majestic spread of eagles' wings
as they soar in morning light.

The beauty of exotic flowers, their vibrant colors while in bloom;
or the cry of a newborn baby
after leaving a mother's womb.

In the exhilarating moment when a climber has reached their goal
of standing on the mountain peak
while gazing at Earth below.

It can happen for the hero on the battlefield of war;
risking their life for others,
their own safety they ignore.

Sometimes our heart just seems to stop and our breath is sucked away
at the passing of a loved one
and the loss we felt that day.

Christ being nailed to the cross in His sacrifice for mankind,
took away His breath while hanging there -
No greater love will we find.

Yes, there are moments in our life that can come any given day,
moments of pleasure or sorrow
that just takes our breath away.

"Who among the gods is like you, O Lord?
Who is like you - majestic in holiness, awesome in glory,
working wonders?"
Exodus 15:11

CAN'T FALL OFF THE FLOOR

When we feel we have failed, with no where to go,
and we feel this deep to the core;
there's no other direction
when we've fallen than upward
'cuz we really can't fall off the floor.

We know when we've reached that low spot in life's journey,
and there's no other direction to go;
we need to stand up
and dust ourselves off
from the floor when we've fallen that low.

Sometimes it may take a trip to that level
for God to show where He wants us to be;
and though it is painful,
and often distressing,
it may take that depth and degree.

Because once we have fallen, we know change must happen;
for "up" is the direction though we're bruised, hurt, and sore.
Sometimes it's a "wake up"
to finally hit rock bottom
'cuz we really can't fall off the floor.

The Lord said to Joshua, "Stand up!
What are you doing down on your face?"
Joshua 7:10

CHASING AFTER WIND

We're running, running, running,
yes, running to and fro.
What we're chasing after we often do not know.

Perhaps we're chasing shadows
that shift and change with light,
or chasing after rainbows with a 'pot of gold' in sight.

Perhaps we're chasing wisdom;
wise choices must be made.
Wisdom can be elusive, but once captured will not fade.

Perhaps we're chasing knowledge,
striving to learn all that we can.
Experience is often better, chasing both should be our plan.

Perhaps we're chasing pleasure;
sometimes right and sometimes wrong.
Like wind it may pass quickly - one minute here, the next it's gone.

Perhaps we're chasing money
and all the wealth that we can hold.
In life there's greater value in the simple things, we're told.

Perhaps we're chasing lifetime goals
and running after dreams.
Our lives often take another course than the ones we've planned, it seems.

Perhaps we're chasing after love,
love we may or may not find.
This one thing please remember, seek a love that's good and kind.

Yes, we can chase after all these things,
like the chasing after wind,
but after all our running, are we satisfied in the end?

I thought to myself, "Look, I have grown and increased in wisdom ..."
Then I applied myself to the understanding of wisdom, and also of madness and folly,
but I learned that this, too, is a chasing after the wind.
Ecclesiastes 1:16-17

CHOICES

Life can be a challenge,
and trials can be strong;
and when we walk our path in life
our choices may be wrong.

But out of every wrong choice,
a lesson can be gained;
and those lessons should be treasured
in the knowledge we've obtained.

We will find God's gentle leading
in the paths we choose to take
though we often stray from that guidance
in the choices that we make.

But we know no matter what we choose,
God's love is always there;
whether our choices may be right or wrong,
and the outcomes seem unfair.

So, welcome all life's choices
on our path that God has laid,
and grasp all that this life offers
knowing wrong choices may be made.

Lead me, O Lord, in your righteousness because of my enemies -
make straight your way before me.
Psalm 5:8

CHOSEN FEW

How many people choose to pray
to a God they do not know?
They wait until disaster strikes
with nowhere else to go.

They quickly fall upon their knees
seeking solace in their prayers,
but do not know to whom they pray,
nor know the God who cares.

It's time for them to realize,
in all they say and do,
they must re-direct their chosen path,
take a path chosen by few.

We shouldn't believe that it's okay
to ignore the God above.
We don't need to live life on our own
when there's a God of love.

Do not wait until heartache comes
when you'll cry out in despair.
There is a God who cares for us -
a God who's always there.

So, be one of the chosen few,
and pray to a God you "know."
Don't wait until disaster strikes,
know now to whom you'll go.

There is one body and one Spirit - just as you were called to
one hope when you were called - one Lord, one faith, one baptism;
one God and Father of all, who is over all and through all and in all.
Ephesians 4:4-6

COME AWAY WITH ME

He sat on the temple steps with the scholars,
saying, "Come away with Me.
Even though I am young, I have plenty to offer;
what I teach, you don't need a degree."

He walked the shores, seeking His disciples,
saying, "Come away with Me.
You have much to learn; you'll be 'fishers of men;'
one day you'll profess My decree."

He gathered the people as they stood on the hill,
saying, "Come away with Me."
He multiplied the fish and increased the bread;
His miracles they plainly could see.

For His miracles were many; His instruction intense,
saying to all, "Come away with Me.
There is no cost for the gift that I offer.
The gift of eternal life is free."

He hung on the cross between two condemned men,
saying, "Come away with Me."
One was willing, the other was not,
while Christ was sacrificed on the tree.

As He was ascending into the eastern sky,
saying, "Come away with Me.
I will return this way again one day.
Be watchful and waiting for me."

Through the Holy Spirit, He softly whispers,
saying, "Come away with Me.
For I am the way, the truth, and the life;
through me I can give you the key."

If you are searching for direction with no place to go,
Christ is calling, "Come away with Me."
Take the path He wants you to follow,
and seek where He wants you to be.

*Jesus answered, "I am the way and the truth and the life.
No one comes to the Father except through me."*
John 14:6

CREATION

God envisioned a perfect world.
So, He decided to create
a world of love and beauty; a place where there's no hate.

He formed the sky and heavens,
the stars and moon and sun;
the Earth and other planets. He's only just begun.

He separated the light and darkness;
divided land and sea.
He created living creatures and all that was to be.

He saw that all His works were good,
but one thing He lacked that day,
someone to govern over all; so, He breathed life into the clay.

"I'll call My creation 'man'," God said,
and saw that it was good.
He was pleased with His creation, but decided that He should -

Also create a helpmate
for this being He called 'man.'
So, He took more clay and one of man's ribs, and completed His perfect plan.

He named man "Adam", the woman "Eve."
In the Garden of Eden they would reside.
They'd care for this place and honor God. All their needs God would provide.

But Satan entered this perfect world,
tempting Adam and Eve, now gone.
The Garden of Eden just a memory. A perfect world gone wrong.

Be thankful that God has forgiven
the wrongs that enter in.
He knows that we are human and forgives us of our sin.

In the beginning God created the heavens and the earth.
Genesis 1:1

DEEP THOUGHTS OF A SHALLOW CHRISTIAN

"There really is no rush today to take the time to pray."
This is how a shallow Christian thinks,
and this is what they'd say:

"Just wait until the car breaks down or you're lost in a blizzard snow,
perhaps when death or sickness strikes
or your team's losing the Super Bowl."

"Wait to pray when a friend is dying or for a relationship gone bad,
perhaps when someone's hurt you
or a friend has made you mad."

"Who has the time to pray anyway as we're rushing through our day.
God already knows our every need,
so why do we need to pray?"

"Does He really want to hear from us when things are going great?
He surely doesn't have time for us
when others' prayers can't wait."

"For God is available twenty-four/seven, three hundred sixty-five days a year.
Do we really need to seek Him
for every disappointment, heartache, fear?"

"Leave the prayers to those who need Him. You don't need to pray every day.
Don't go to Him with your needless prayers,"
is what a shallow Christian would say.

But Jesus says, "Seek and you will find. Knock and I will be there.
In everything, please come to Me
through supplication and through prayer."

Let's not be that shallow Christian, thinking there's no real need to pray.
Speak to Jesus in all situations.
He wants to hear what we have to say!

Do not be anxious about anything, but in everything,
by prayer and petition, with thanksgiving, present your requests to God.
Philippians 4:6

DON'T JUDGE

The old man said, "Please help me;
I'm homeless don't you know.
I'm wandering the streets on this cold winter night,
and you turn away and say no."

"I know you think I'm drunk or an addict,
and, yes, perhaps that I am,
but that doesn't mean that I'm not hungry or cold,
or not in a financial jam."

"Should you be so judgmental
that you think I'll go buy a beer
or drugs to support my habit?
I just might, you may be right, I fear."

"But God knows my every current need,
and He places the love in your heart
to help those of us who need a hand,
and your show of deep caring plays a part."

"Look beyond what I may use the handout for.
Don't judge where the money goes.
Let God in heaven be the final judge,
for the intent, on both parts, He knows."

"So, don't hesitate to give a buck or two
to help your fellow man.
We just might be angels in disguise,
and your giving may be part of God's plan!"

"Do not judge, or you too will be judged."
Matthew 7:1

DON'T LET THE SUN GO DOWN TODAY

Don't let the sun go down today
before you've righted any wrong;
before apologizing for any anger
though that anger may be strong.

Don't let the sun go down today
before making all wrongs right;
before seeking the lost and lonely,
and helping others see God's light.

Don't let the sun go down today
before helping those who are weak;
or visiting seniors and those in jail,
and any others you should seek.

Don't let the sun go down today
before helping your fellow man;
before feeding the hungry and helping the poor,
and doing all that you can.

Don't let the sun go down today
on your anger and your wrath,
for you will be blessed and rest in peace
when you follow this lighted path.

For once the sun has gone down today
and you're no longer in the light,
if you've let the world control you,
you've lost the chance to make wrongs "right."

Forgive and be forgiven.
Quiet any anger in your mind.
And before the sun goes down today,
true peace is what you'll find!

"In your anger do not sin":
Do not let the sun go down while you are still angry ...
Ephesians 4:26

DOUBTING THOMAS

He heard about the healings,
the lame could walk, the blind could see.
He heard about the miracles
along the Sea of Galilee.

He was one of the disciples,
and he tried hard to perceive,
but his faith was based on sight and touch
for him to thoroughly believe.

Jesus though wanted total trust
in the things one cannot see;
in things of which one cannot touch,
to truly be "doubt" free.

But Thomas doubted within his mind
the miracles before him now.
How could this Jesus heal the sick and blind,
and be raised from the grave somehow?

But Jesus knows of our doubtful minds,
and, like Thomas, we may struggle too.
Jesus wants us to reach out and touch His wounds
to know what He's done for you.

Reach out and touch the wounds of Christ,
and wipe away uncertainty from your mind.
Know that you can trust and believe,
leaving all sins and doubts behind!

Then he said to Thomas, "Put your finger here; see my hands.
Reach out your hand and put it into my side.
Stop doubting and believe."
John 20:27

DRAGGING GOD WITH US

We often just blindly forge ahead
not giving a thought to God,
and what His plans may be for us
though our own plans may be flawed.

We make decisions, we move ahead,
without taking time to think twice;
and then we search for His blessings
when we first should have sought His advice.

We often drag God along with us
in our "have-to-do-it-now" pace;
without first seeking His guidance
or checking that it's blessed with His grace.

We should always first check with the Father;
submit to His guidance instead.
Let Him be the one doing the dragging
and lead us where He wants us to tread.

God's plans will always be better;
they'll always be just what we need.
We must surrender our lives to the Father,
and let Him take over and lead!

For this God is our God forever and ever;
he will be our guide even to the end.
Psalm 48:14

DRAW ME NEARER, LORD

Draw me nearer, Lord,
to thy precious side.
A side that was cruelly pierced;
a wound you could not hide.

Draw me nearer, Lord,
to the foot of the tree.
A tree that served as a rough-hewn cross
on which you died for me.

Draw me nearer, Lord,
to the door of your grave.
A tomb where the stone was rolled away;
resurrection of the life you gave.

Draw me nearer, Lord,
to the foot of the throne.
The seat of the Almighty God
of which is our future "home."

Draw me nearer, Lord,
nearer only to you.
Show me the way that I must go
and the things that I must do.

Jesus answered, "I am the way and the truth and the life.
No one comes to the Father except through me."
John 14:6

DROP THE FISHING NETS

If I were on the fishing boat with the nets that I did mend,
and Jesus said "Just leave them,"
would I go where He would send?

Would I have dropped the fishing nets? Would I have just walked away
from the work that I was doing
to follow the Lord that day?

Would I have worried about tomorrow?
Concerned with family and life's cares?
Who would earn my keep and pay my bills,
and handle all my affairs?

And what about my life today? Do I go where He does send?
Do I give up all and follow Him,
and trust Him as my friend?

Do I let my earthly wants and needs cloud the greatest gift of all;
not seeking His grace and mercy,
nor listening to His call?

When He says, "Drop what you're doing - walk away from what you've got."
Am I trusting this man who died for me;
dropping "all" right on the spot?

Help me drop my heavy fishing nets. Help me, Lord, just walk away
from all that this world offers.
Help me find my place, I pray.

Knowing my place is always with you … trusting you as God's dear Son.
Help me give up all that I hold dear
in light of all you've done.

"Come, follow me," Jesus said,
"and I will make you fishers of men."
Matthew 4:19

DYING

Dying is part of living;
it's just another stage.
It can happen in an instant,
no matter what your age.

It shouldn't be something fearful
causing stress and dreaded so.
Especially as a Christian,
you know where you're going to go.

Yes, it can happen all the sudden
to both the young and old,
but when passing through death's valley
angels are with you, I am told.

So, don't fret at the thought of dying.
It's just another day.
Perhaps in another place and time,
but was lovingly planned that way.

Life in the next stage is much better;
no sickness, sorrow, strife.
Though final to those you leave behind;
for you a better life.

Dying is part of living;
it's just another stage.
But you must be ever ready,
no matter what your age.

Here is a trustworthy saying:
If we died with him, we will also live with him …
2 Timothy 2:11

EVERY

Every minute of every hour
of every day, Lord, belongs to you.
For you are there in every moment
of every task I daily do.

Every prayer for every lost soul
of every person who comes to me,
will be answered by you, dear Father,
for you hear my every plea.

Every burden of every wrong choice,
and every sin that I have made,
will be cleansed by your blood and mercy,
and your grace will be displayed.

Every pulse of every heartbeat
and every motion my body makes
are daily blessed and sanctioned by you
in each and every breath I take.

Every tear from joys and sorrow,
and every heartache that comes my way,
I know you'll take and claim each tear, Lord,
to place within my crown one day.

Every note and every chorus
of every song of praise I do
is truly the greatest form of worship
in raising up my love to you!

*Every good and perfect gift is from above,
coming from the Father of the heavenly lights,
who does not change like shifting shadows.*
James 1:17

EVERY TEAR

Every tear that falls is precious
to the Lord our God and King,
and He preserves each in a bottle
with the memories that they bring.

He remembers each occasion
for every single tear you've shed;
knows each sorrow and each heartache
in this earthly life you've led.

He knows the tears of every baby,
every cut and scuffed-up knee.
He knows the tears of your hurt feelings
when you thought no one would see.

Tears when you didn't make the team,
when kids didn't pick you for their game;
when your behavior was a disappointment,
and you bowed your head in shame.

Every time your parents argued
and you tried to plug your ears,
or the death of your beloved
and the flowing of healing tears.

Tears when Grandma no longer remembers you
or your best friend has moved away;
perhaps a damaged, broken, marriage
or a love that's gone astray.

For every single tear that's fallen,
God catches each within His Hands
and stores them in a treasured bottle
'til the settling of life's sands.

When life's hourglass sands are finished,
sifting slowly, falling down,
every tear He placed in that bottle
are now diamonds for your crown!

Record my lament;
list my tears on your scroll - are they not in your record?
Psalm 56:8

FAITH, HOPE, AND LOVE

Where is my heart, Lord?
Where have I left it?
Where have I shared it along the way?
Sometimes it is battered,
sometimes it is broken,
but I'm willing to give it as I trust and obey.

Where is my strength, Lord?
Where have I left it?
Often, I'm tired with no more to give.
Sometimes I am weak,
sometimes I am weary,
seeking your power, though, each day that I live.

Where is my faith, Lord?
Where have I left it?
Where is the stronghold I know is in you?
Sometimes I am doubtful,
sometimes life consumes me,
help me remember you're trustworthy and true.

Where is my hope, Lord?
Where have I left it?
Have I pushed all my hopes and dreams to the side?
Sometimes hope has faded,
sometimes it has vanished,
renew in me vision not to let dreams subside.

Where is the love, Lord?
Where have I left it?
Have I given out all the love one can hold?
Sometimes love is fleeting,
sometimes I embrace it,
help me to share it with a passion untold.

Help me reach out, Lord,
with arms that are yearning
for the faith, hope, and love that you willingly give.
Help me accept
and receive all your blessings,
sharing them with others in this life that we live.

And now these three remain: faith, hope and love.
But the greatest of these is love.
1 Corinthians 13:13

FORGIVENESS

What's the difference you may ask
between a hard place and a rock?
Is it the imaginary wall before you
blocking the pathway that you walk?

It is the anger you feel toward a loved one
or prejudice that has been ingrained?
Is it the grudge that you have harbored
toward a friend who has caused you pain?

Is it the wrongs that have been inflicted
upon your spirit from time to time
or the mountains of rejection
you are daily forced to climb?

Is it the bitterness and denials
in the life that's been your due;
the resentment you've allowed to multiply
with the hardships handed you?

Do you think the hard place would soften
if you forgave the burdens that you bear?
Would the rocks and boulders in your pathway
turn to sand with fervent prayer?

Forgiveness can be a mighty thing
full of mercy and saving grace.
It can be the perfect solution,
granting peace in all you face.

So, when you're between a rock and hard place
and bitter grievances are in the way,
pardon those many burdensome grudges;
forgiving now. Do not delay!

Bear with each other and forgive whatever grievances
you may have against one another.
Forgive as the Lord forgave you.
Colossians 3:13

FORGIVENESS AND GRACE

A new chapter in your book of life
while living upon this Earth.
A cleansing that washes away all sin;
a renewal and rebirth.

Giving your life to the Father,
let the sacred waters flow,
a baptism of repentance
with this cleansing of the soul.

A time for the Holy Spirit,
a calling deep within
to seek the Father's blessings
and forgiveness of your sin.

Rising up from the immersion,
with joy within your heart;
you sense rededication
to the new life about to start.

When you rise up from the water
and feel the fresh air on your face,
you know something special has happened;
now blessed with forgiveness and grace.

You have washed away your old life,
you're now starting life anew.
No matter what life now hands out
God is always there for you!

And so John came, baptizing in the desert region
and preaching a baptism of repentance for the
forgiveness of sins.
Mark 1:4

FORGIVING

It's hard to forgive our fellow man
when they have done us wrong.
Three little words, "I am sorry,"
so simple and yet so strong,
are difficult to utter
when they, themselves, should say
these very words for the hurt they've caused
and the price we've had to pay.

But God expects us to forget;
to move beyond the hate.
To love our enemies as ourselves,
and, in so doing, relate.
To forgive and be forgiven,
if only for God's sake,
for He is the one we must honor
in this world of give and take.
In knowing that He forgives us
of all the wrongs that we have done,
we, too, must forgive others
as instructed by God's Son!

"Do not judge, and you will not be judged.
Do not condemn, and you will not be condemned.
Forgive, and you will be forgiven."
Luke 6:37

FREEDOM

Where does freedom really begin;
where does it really start?
Is it just a fancy byword;
does it begin within the heart?

Does freedom mean not being a slave;
placing all concerns on a shelf?
Does it mean not being accountable
to anyone but yourself?

Is freedom just a matter of speech;
the right to have your say?
The right to make it known to all
that you must always have your way?

We all have chains that bind us.
Are any of us really free
to break these binding restrictions?
One really must take time to see.

That it's not just a fancy byword;
it's not being no slave to one;
it's not being free from worry;
it's believing in God's only Son.

Read God's Holy Bible daily;
you'll surely find freedom there.
Where the Spirit is - there is freedom,
and its freedom you should share.

Where does freedom really begin;
where does it really start?
It's not just a fancy byword.
It begins within your heart!

Now the Lord is the Spirit,
and where the Spirit of the Lord is, there is freedom.
2 Corinthians 3:17

GETTING EVEN

People push and people shove
just to get ahead;
they only think of just themselves
not caring on whom they tread.
Getting even is all they think
when someone does them in;
they don't stop to contemplate
that you have called it "sin."
And sometimes we just wish, dear Lord,
in turning the other cheek,
that we wouldn't have to turn so often;
you know our flesh is weak.
You tell us to walk that extra mile;
not one, but take on two.
My shoes are dusty and my feet are tired,
but I know you've walked them too.
I can't help it, Lord, but I get hurt
when others do me wrong;
like them, I want to just strike back.
Please help me to be strong.
Deep inside our human nature
we are all alike, you see;
and you knew this when you came to die
upon that rough-hewn tree.
Getting even, Lord, is not your way;
you taught us this in life.
Help us not to want revenge
and cause some spiritual strife.
Help us, Lord, to know the difference
of standing up for what we believe,
or just getting back at someone
who has caused our soul to grieve.
Give us patience and understanding;
spiritual loving deep within
of our fellow human brothers
in this world we must live in.

A man's wisdom gives him patience;
it is to his glory to overlook an offense.
Proverbs 19:11

GIFT OF GRACE

You know, dear Lord, I intended
to do good works today,
but something blocked my intentions
of what I meant to do and say.

I feel I didn't measure up
to the standards I set for me.
How could I be so terribly remiss
in what I do for Thee?

Us humans feel to be worthy
we must measure by good deeds.
We weary ourselves in our busyness
to fulfill our righteous needs.

But you state our deeds are as "filthy rags,"
sinners no matter what we do;
and the only way to true salvation
is by trust and faith in you.

Please help us, Lord, to accept your grace
and to fully trust in your love;
Stop measuring ourselves by our good works,
but place our hopes in things above.

Thank you for your forgiveness, Lord.
Help us to accept your gift of grace.
Help us to seek repentance
and salvation's firm embrace.

*All of us have become like one who is unclean,
and all of our righteous acts are like filthy rags ...*
Isaiah 64:6

GIVING

As I dropped my money in the offering plate
on its way on down the aisle,
I asked myself, "Am I giving my all"
as I passed it on with a smile?
Am I giving my all in other ways,
not just money tossed in the plate?
Do I listen with my heart to those in need
and give love to those who hate?
Giving is much better than taking,
and we should make it our daily task
to take time to count on what we can give
than to list things for which we could ask.
Our lives would certainly be more blessed
with many benefits to achieve
when we take the focus off ourselves
and give more than we receive.
Let it be our mission
to be more giving every day,
and to put aside our own worthless "wants"
and give of ourselves in every way!

*In everything I did, I showed you that by this kind
of hard work we must help the weak, remembering
the words the Lord Jesus Himself said:
"It is more blessed to give than to receive."*
Acts 20:35

GIVING OUR ALL

We give and give and give and give,
'til we can't give any more,
and then we just turn right around
and give more than before.

Sometimes it seems it's not enough
when we've given all we've got,
but we seem to keep on giving
in our desire to share our lot.

We give our money when we can,
though there never seems enough
for all the things that come our way,
especially when times are tough.

We freely give away our time,
though it quickly slips away,
like sand passing through an hourglass
in a swift, relentless, way.

We give our friendship even when
some friends don't seem to care,
but we surely want our closest friends
to know we're always there.

We give away our deepest love,
even though love's often blind.
Who truly knows the ways of the heart
when dealing with ties that bind?

May we always strive to give away
what we're able to when we can.
That our hearts be always open
to the "giving" in God's plan.

Give generously to him and do so without a grudging heart;
then because of this the Lord your God will bless you
in all your work and in everything you put your hand to.
Deuteronomy 15:10

GO OUT IN DEEP WATER

Go out in deep water.
Be fishers of men.
Lead others to Christ and then do it again.

Don't stop 'til you're tired,
you're weak, and you're sore.
Go out in those waters. Don't stand on the shore.

There's a place of salvation
where all men can be,
but some must be led, for they're blind 'til they see.

As servants, we must lead them,
for their lives are at stake;
though waves may be daunting, and we tremble and quake.

Don't be frightened and weary.
No, don't be afraid;
for God is there with us in waters we wade.

Seeking the lonely,
the tired, the lost,
as we tread through life's waters, knowing Christ paid the cost.

That salvation is there
as we show each the way.
Yes, go out in deep water, just trust and obey.

When he had finished speaking, he said to Simon,
"Put out into deep water, and let down the nets for a catch."
Luke 5:4

Then Jesus said ... "Don't be afraid;
from now on you will catch men."
Luke 5:10

GOD IS THERE

When you were born, and you took your first breath,
and your gasping cries filled the air;
you may have felt you were all alone.
Please know, though, that God was there.

When you were a toddler and took your first steps,
and your unsteadiness created quite a scare;
you may have felt you were all alone.
Please know, though, that God was there.

When you were a teen and out with your friends;
staying out late 'cause your parents did not care;
you may have felt you were all alone.
Please know, though, that God was there.

When you become an adult – raising kids, paying bills,
and your dreams no one seems to share;
you may feel that you are all alone.
Please know, though, that God is there.

When the years go by, and the kids leave home;
your life filled with isolation and despair;
you may feel that you are all alone.
Please know, though, that God is there.

Though physically tired and weary of soul,
and you don't feel like bowing in prayer;
you may feel that you are all alone.
Please know, though, that God is there.

When you consider your life that you wish would just end,
a life you do not wish to spare,
you may feel that you are all alone.
Please know, though, that God is there.

"And surely I will be with you always,
to the very end of the age."
Matthew 28:20

GOD WHISPERED

God whispered in my ear today,
"What have you done for Me?
Have you shared with others the Gospel and helped the spiritually blind to see?"

God whispered in my ear today
when seeing homeless on the street,
"Clothe and find them lodging, and give them food to eat."

God whispered in my ear today
while watching my fellow man,
"Always be ready and willing, with compassion, to lend a hand."

God whispered in my ear today
when I heard a baby cry,
"Love the little children for, through them, My Kingdom is nigh."

God whispered in my ear today
while viewing flowers in full bloom,
"The world is full of My beauty, not just evil, death, and gloom."

God whispered in my ear today
while going my hectic pace,
"Stop and seek My solace for, through Me, is amazing grace."

God whispered in my ear today
while on my knees to pray,
"Lead others to the holy cross; I'll help you show the way."

God whispered in my ear today,
"Take time to hear My voice;
tell others of My salvation; let them know they have a choice."

God whispered in my ear today,
"Well done, My faithful friend,
you've done the things I've asked of you. You went where I did send."

"What I tell you in the dark, speak in the daylight;
what is whispered in your ear,
proclaim from the housetops."
Matthew 10:27

GOD'S GALAXY

The Earth moves on its axis
ever sure and ever slow,
but times are always changing
in this planet that we know.

God is never changing,
always there both firm and strong.
The Earth will keep on spinning
with its chaos right and wrong.

But true peace is in God's orbit,
which surpasses time and space.
The Earth can keep on spinning,
but our sphere rests in God's grace.

So as the Earth moves forward
in this galaxy God designed,
we should follow, like a comet,
in God's orbit most divine!

But God made the earth by his power;
he founded the world by his wisdom
and stretched out the heavens by his understanding.
Jeremiah 10:12

GOD'S LOVE

When we feel the wind against our face,
we can feel God's gentle touch;
He lets us know He's by our side
and loves us very much.

The wind may be soft and gentle,
or strongly rustling through the trees;
for surely all of nature feels
God's love within that breeze.

We may not understand such love;
a love we don't deserve.
The love that He bestows on us,
He gives without reserve.

We may fail in our daily walk,
even failing those we love;
to them we may never be good enough,
nor measure up to God above.

But we can know that in our failings,
God's love is always here;
we can feel Him in our surroundings
and just know He's always near.

And when we feel that gentle wind;
the cool breeze against our tears,
we know we have all we'll ever need,
and fear and doubt disappears.

He gives to us unconditional love;
always giving to me and you.
We can feel God's touch in the gentle breeze ...
A love that's real and true.

This is love: not that we loved God, but that He loved us
and sent His Son as an atoning sacrifice for our sins.
1 John 4:10

GOD'S MIGHTY VOICE

As thunder rumbles in the distance,
God's mighty voice is heard;
to some it's fear and danger - to others love assured.

As it rolls across the valley,
proclaiming God's mighty power,
it brings a sense of comfort in His time and in His hour.

His mighty power flashes,
lighting up the evening sky,
preceding the roll of thunder, majestic to the eye.

The breeze whispers of His greatness;
His mightiness in the wind;
it can either comfort or destroy - depending on man's sin.

What God is trying to tell us
through His message of today,
He speaks to us through nature, His majesty to portray.

His love is also written
across the sky in color form,
proclaiming through the rainbow His promise from the storm.

So, if in today's tense world
you feel God is no longer around,
just listen to all of nature. His presence does abound.

Listen to the thunder
as it rolls across the way;
stand in awe of the wind and lightning. Listen to what God has to say.

When he thunders, the waters in the heavens roar;
he makes clouds rise from the ends of the earth.
He sends lightning with the rain and
brings out the wind from his storehouses.
Jeremiah 51:16

GOD'S PAINTING OUR PORTRAIT

God's painting our portrait
and what does one see
on the canvas before Him as He paints you and me?

Are we frowning or smiling;
looking up or gazing down?
Is there hope in our smile or despair in our frown?

Is our face brightened by wisdom;
softened by the warm glow
of our hope in the Savior and His grace that we know?

Does our pose show us praying,
sitting quiet and still?
Are we portrayed serving others in our mission to fulfill?

Are our hands gladly clapping,
or perhaps lifted in praise,
thanking God for His mercy as we live out our days?

Are we clothed in compassion,
being gentle and kind,
with our attitude spotless, no stains there to find?

And what is the setting
of this portrait we're in?
Is it lit by God's love and His forgiveness of sin?

I'm sure that our portrait
will be radiant and bright
as God paints with vibrant colors and we smile in His light.

On this canvas before Him
He has painted with flair
the life we are living with His love portrayed there.

"In the same way, let your light shine before men,
that they may see your good deeds
and praise your Father in heaven."
Matthew 5:16

GOD'S PLAN

Just when the plans you thought were great
and were given much thought and care,
they were quickly ripped from within your grasp
even after giving them much prayer.

You cried, "Did God not hear my petition;
could He not know my plea?
Surely God can see my inner needs
and know what's right for me!"

You prayed that your plans would be answered
just the way you knew that they should,
but it's just not turning out that way.
God could make it so, if He would.

It often seems like mere silence
when asking God to respond.
And in our fast-paced planning,
God's answers just take too long.

And when the answer is forthcoming,
and you know it's not going to be
the answer you hoped and prayed for,
you cry out, "Dear Lord, why me?"

Please know that looking in hindsight
you will find God knew all along
the best path for your plans to have taken,
and your hopes and desires were wrong.

Your prayer should be for the wisdom and strength
to accept His answer and call;
to follow the path He has planned for you.
Be prepared to give Him your all.

Many are the plans in a man's heart,
but it is the Lord's purpose that prevails.
Proverbs 19:21

GOD'S SHIELD

Is there evil lurking
just around the corner's bend?
Hiding there and waiting,
ever ready to descend?

What happened to the morals
that were taught us in our youth?
It seems that they are long gone,
tragic lies replacing truth.

It seems that evil's promoted;
every single wrong deemed right.
Yes, evil's around the corner,
we must raise God's shield and fight.

It's attacking our homes and families,
finances and religion too;
and if you're not keenly ready
will surely attack even you.

Yes, evil's around the corner,
just waiting to pounce and fight.
Be ready with God's shield.
Raise that shield and do what's right!

In addition to all this, take up the shield of faith,
with which you can extinguish all the flaming
arrows of the evil one.
Ephesians 6:16

GPS

You do not need a GPS
when trying to find your way,
as you have Jesus as your guide
to direct your paths each day.

He alone is your guidance system
in your global-positioning quest;
you just have to plug into Jesus,
and He will take care of the rest.

You don't have to worry at getting lost
or taking the wrong way home;
just trust in His guidance and wisdom,
and know that you're never alone.

If you're feeling lost in life's travels,
and your directions seem all a mess;
you will reach your designation.
Just let Jesus be your GPS!

*Jesus answered, "I am the way and the truth
and the life. No one comes to the Father
except through me."*
John 14:6

GRACE-FILLED LOVE

We know that at our weakest,
Christ's grace is there for us.
We feel His mighty power and strength,
and in Him we can trust.

His grace is always sufficient
at the time we need His power.
Made perfect in our weakness
any time of day or hour.

We may suffer physical ailments,
loss of loved ones or a job;
perhaps stress in our relationships
or a separation from our God.

But when we pray to find the answers
to the challenges of our day,
His grace-filled love surrounds us;
His perfect power will not sway.

For when we're at our weakest
and everything seems wrong,
Christ's love and power rests on us,
and it's then that we are strong!

But he said to me, "My grace is sufficient for you,
for my power is made perfect in weakness."
Therefore I will boast all the more gladly about my weaknesses,
so that Christ's power may rest on me.
2 Corinthians 12:9

GRACELAND

There is a place for each of us;
a place we each can go.
A land of love, forgiveness, peace,
where mercy and grace flow.

God sends us there with all His love
when He forgives our sin.
Forgiveness came upon the cross,
our ticket to enter in.

With His one and only beloved Son
we travel to this place.
He takes us from the darkest path,
placing us within His grace.

He knows our human frailness.
He knows our wants and needs.
He'll walk with us along the way,
regardless of our deeds.

No other experience can describe
the day He takes our hand
and leads us to that marvelous place
described as His "Graceland!"

For it is by grace you have been saved, through faith -
and this not from yourselves, it is the gift of God -
not by works, so that no one can boast.
Ephesians 2:8-9

GUIDANCE

I love the Lord Jesus.
He means so much to me.
He leads me where no one else goes.
He leads and I follow,
He knows I am waiting
for the guidance He lovingly shows.

I long for instruction
from our kind, loving Savior.
The lessons He's willing to give.
But my heart must be open,
my mind most receptive
to learn how He wants me to live.

The world's ever changing;
fast-paced and in motion.
No time to really stand still.
But the Savior is knocking.
You must always be ready
to accept His grace and His will!

"Here I am! I stand at the door and knock.
If anyone hears my voice and opens the door,
I will come in and eat with him, and he with me."
Revelations 3:20

HE IS THE LORD

He is Lord,
the mighty God of Heaven.
He is the Lord,
our mighty King.
He is the Lord,
in this world we live in,
and Lord of everything.

He is the Son
of God the Father.
He is the Son
who came to Earth.
He is the Son,
not judging but rather
to give new life and re-birth.

He is the Savior
whom we should worship.
He is the Savior
for all of time.
He is the Savior
who in all kinship
saved us from death and sin's crime.

Now praise the King
for all He has done.
Now praise the King
for all of His gifts.
Now praise the King,
the risen Savior,
our hearts and souls He joyfully lifts!

I will give thanks to the Lord because of his
righteousness and will sing praise to the
name of the Lord Most High.
Psalm 7:17

HE IS THERE

When we stumble on the narrow path, not giving our walk much care,
nor seeing the road blocks in our way,
we know that He is there.

We may often be too busy in our hurry-up world for prayer;
not taking the time we know we should
but we know that He is there.

When we take on all life's challenges, taking risks we shouldn't dare;
not knowing whether we'll win or lose,
we'll always know that He's there.

When others are in desperate need and we give all we can share,
and we feel we've given all we've got,
we'll know that He is there.

When we daily laugh and sing and dance, living life with special flair,
and peace has settled within our soul,
we'll surely know He's there.

Every time our heart is broken and our spirit is in despair,
we may feel like no one understands,
we know though that He's there.

When we've walked through the valley of the shadow of death
and we shout that life's not fair,
we may feel abandoned and alone
but we know He's always there.

When our days are done and over, with gray sprinkled throughout our hair,
and we've finished our walk upon this Earth,
we'll know that He is there.

And when we've reached the Pearly Gates after climbing Heaven's stair,
we will see the golden Throne of God
and know that He is there!

The Lord is in his holy temple;
the Lord is on his heavenly throne.
He observes the sons of men;
his eyes examine them.
Psalm 11:4

HEALING TEARS

Tears fall from our eyes through emotions of life,
through joy, laughter, heartache, and pain.
There's healing power within each one that falls
and strength from each one that you'll gain.

You might just hold back from shedding those tears
thinking it isn't the strong way to be,
but tears are a natural occurrence in life
and you really should let them fall free.

They wash away sorrows that build up inside
and cleanse the hurt feelings within;
they'll release the anxieties of life's doubts and fears,
and in them true healing will begin.

Tears may fall when you're spending some time with a friend
in the laughter and sorrows you share.
Tears may fall when you experience tough times in your life
or when pouring your heart out in prayer.

Jesus knew of the importance of releasing those tears
for He, too, shed some tears for mankind.
He knew tears would heal the body and soul,
and the freedom in them that you'll find.

So, let those tears fall when they come to your eyes;
don't hold them back anymore.
For there's healing power within each one that falls,
and that's what God created them for.

Jesus wept.
John 11:35

HEAVEN'S GATE

Who's the keeper of the door awaiting at Heaven's Gate?
There's many who could be waiting,
parent, teacher, minister, mate.

There are your loving parents who guided you through the years.
They were there for all your wants and needs,
and there to soothe your fears.

There are the educators who taught you along the way.
Their hopes and dreams were centered
on the success you'd be one day.

There are the various pastors who ministered to heart and soul.
Aiming you upwards toward the pearly gate
was their one main, selfless, goal.

And what about the doctors who administered your physical needs;
were there in times of sickness and health
tending to their medicinal deeds.

And then, of course, would be your mate who always knew just what to do.
They'd be waiting there by Heaven's door;
arms outstretched waiting there for you.

And there would be your family and friends, associates, co-workers and such.
All will be rejoicing your arrival;
perhaps, unknowing, they loved you much.

But the one true face you'll long to see will surely be standing in place
at the center of Heaven's pearly doors,
tears of joy flowing down His face.

Earth's journey has ended at this door; you've traversed life's well-traveled road.
You'll be entering eternity with Jesus;
eased of Earth's weary time-laden load!

He was afraid and said, "How awesome is this place!
This is none other than the house of God;
this is the gate of heaven."
Genesis 28:17

HOPE NOT IN WEALTH

What does one do when they're moving on
to another time and place?
They've had enough of the same old thing
and need a change of pace.

When the goals and dreams they're after
always seem just out of range,
and they never seem to move ahead …
they'll know it's time for change.

Perhaps they need new dreams and goals.
On life's path they have stepped out of line.
They've become sidetracked in their journey to wealth
on a road wasting money and time.

Perhaps their heart is in the wrong place.
They're hoping for what should not be.
They're constantly striving for riches and wealth,
true riches they just cannot see.

Place all of your hopes not in wealth, but in God,
who provides for all of your needs.
Strive to do good and be willing to share,
and be "rich" in doing good deeds.

Always strive to do your best;
giving all in what you set out to do.
Praise the Lord for all that you have
and riches will come to you.

Command those who are rich in this present world
not to be arrogant nor to put their hope in wealth,
which is so uncertain, but to put their hope in God,
who richly provides us with everything
for our enjoyment.
1 Timothy 6:17

HOW CAN YOU

How can you say that you have faith
and profess that's how you feel,
if you've never put it to the test
nor believe things unseen are real?

How can you say that you have hope
while letting worries get in the way;
allowing doubts to block your dreams;
not setting goals each day?

How can you say that you have love
when hate is in your heart?
You're to love your neighbor as yourself,
and ridding hate would be a start.

How can you say you fully trust,
but then do things on your own;
not fully giving up your all,
and your defiant will is shown?

How can you walk upon this Earth
and not truly be amazed
of all that God has done for you
throughout your life and days?

Show others that you do have faith
and hope and trust and love,
and truly believe your life is led
by the hand of God above.

Then Jesus told him, "Because you have seen me,
you have believed; blessed are those who have not seen
and yet have believed."
John 20:29

HOW MANY?

How many breaks before a heart's truly broken?
How many tears fall before running dry?
How many lonely nights before love's forgotten?
How many rejections when you no longer try?

How many arguments when you no longer listen?
How many silences before someone seems gone?
How many hurts before sad songs are written
about a life of love that's gone wrong?

How many warnings before they are heeded?
How many relationships have you slighted and snubbed?
How many longings before one feels needed?
How many hugs before feeling you're loved?

How many burdens before no longer standing?
How many punches before striking back?
How many surrenders before becoming demanding?
How much can one "give" before feeling the lack?

How many pains before truly aching?
How many bruises before healing begins?
How many nights of tossing and turning
among all the pleadings for forgiveness of sins?

How many wars before peace is granted?
How many "I'm sorrys" before you forgive?
How many testings before being trusted?
How many trials before you can live?

How many goals before truly achieving?
How many dreams have you pushed to the side?
How much of "seeing" is truly believing?
How many lost dreams over which have you cried?

How many achievements before feeling successful?
How many pats on the back does one need?
How many cautions before being careful?
How long will you follow before you will lead?

How many prayers do you feel must be uttered?
How many pleas before God hears your prayers?
How many appeals do you feel must be mustered
before turning to God with your doubts and your cares?

Then Peter came to Jesus and asked, "Lord, how many times
shall I forgive my brother when he sins against me?
Up to seven times?"
Jesus answered, "I tell you, not seven times, but seventy-seven times."
Matthew 18:21-22

HUMANITY

You ask me if he's black, white, or tan …
within my sight, it matters not, I know.
For it's what is within man's inner being
and the personal qualities that show.

All of us must inhabit this Earth together
regardless of the differences among us abound.
We're here to live upon this Earth as brothers …
God hopes His Holy Spirit, within each, is found.

Let's destroy the barriers and fences that are constructed
to separate mankind from all that is right;
knowing that to live within God's righteous kingdom,
we must become blind to receive unbiased sight.

Love people of all nationalities, race, and color,
and shake the dust of prejudicial dirt behind.
Pass on to higher levels of reconciled devotion
and grasp the inner sanctum of God's will for mankind.

Raise your hands in praise toward Heaven together,
as one body, which God would have us all be.
Pray that all nations may inhabit this fine Earth;
living together in rich humanity!

You are all sons of God through faith in Christ Jesus …
There is neither Jew nor Greek, slave nor free,
male nor female, for you are all one in Christ Jesus.
Galatians 3:26-27

I AM A GOOD PERSON

I am a good person;
I want you to know,
with a heart and a mind
and a body and soul.

I've had a few failures;
a few hard knocks in life,
and maybe haven't handled well
life's stresses and strife.

I may have been down
and out on skid row,
but I'm still a human being
who sometimes loses control.

With help from good people
I'll get back on my feet,
to move forward, move onward;
not accepting defeat.

My goal in this life
is to stand tall and be strong.
No matter where life takes me
I can never go wrong.

If I just tell myself
that, in life, all I need
is confidence, self-respect,
and a will to succeed.

I am a good person.
Don't doubt what I know.
I'll just hold my head high
and go with life's flow!

*"The good man brings good things out of the good
stored up in his heart ..."*
Luke 6:45

I DEARLY LOVE YOU

"I dearly love you," Jesus said, as He stretched His arms out wide
with the spiky thorns upon His head
and the spear wound through His side.

"I've come to show you real love, as the Father has loved Me.
To come to Earth to live and die,
and to hang upon this tree."

"I came that I could truly know each and every sin you face
as you live throughout your daily lives
in this sinful, worldly place."

"I know each sorrow and heartache that you experience each day.
I know the joy and laughter
in the things you do and say."

"I know each and every temptation as I, too, was tempted here
and for all these many reasons,
I hold you near and dear."

"I know the stress of illness of body, soul, and mind.
Regardless of the outcome,
I know the peace you'll find."

"Yes, I dearly and truly love you, and now know what you go through
as you walk upon your earthly path
and the daily things you do."

"I want you to know the Father and His love for all mankind.
With love, He sent Me to you
and, through Me, true love you'll find!"

"As the Father has loved me, so have I loved you.
Now remain in my love."
John 15:9

I HEAR GOD'S VOICE

I hear God's voice whispering
but it's not within my ear,
it's within my inner being;
not a sound that one can hear.

It's not in the distant thunder
or the rushing of a stream,
nor in the gentle breezes
or the light of bright moonbeam.

Though in all of these His presence
is felt and seen around.
It's within our inner Spirit
where His mighty voice is found.

You can hear His loving instructions
telling each of us right from wrong.
You've always called it intuition
when it's been God's voice all along.

So, when you have to make a choice,
don't listen with your ear.
Just listen with the Spirit,
and you'll hear what you need to hear.

God's voice thunders in marvelous ways;
he does great things beyond our understanding.
Job 37:5

I VISITED WITH GOD

I visited with God today.
In disbelief, you ask me how.
He gives us each a special gift,
and I'll share it with you now.

In Noah's Day, and Moses' too,
His visits were more direct.
But as time went on and things had changed,
it's through the Bible that we connect.

God, in His infinite wisdom,
knew we would need His Living Word
and the guidance among the pages
is sharper than any two-edged sword.

In it, He gives us wisdom,
assurance, strength, and love;
and the way we can receive these
is through the words of God above.

If you will take the time in reading
what this special book has to say,
you will know that God is speaking
to you, through it, every day.

Take the time to visit
with our Father and our Friend,
for He is truly speaking
from beginning page to the end.

For the word of God is living and active.
Sharper than any double-edged sword ..."
Hebrews 4:12

I WANT

I want laughter when life is funny.
I want music throughout my day.
I want peace when life seems troubled
and answers when I pray.

I want thunder when it's raining.
I want night-time stars to glow.
I want beauty in every sunrise
and, on Christmas, soft white snow.

I want hugs when touch is needed.
I want love straight from the heart.
I want strong arms when I'm weary
and be missed when we're apart.

I want wisdom when I'm speaking.
I want passion in all I do.
I want truth when truth is needed
and inner strength to see me through.

I want to hear words unspoken.
I want to sense another's pain.
I want to help where need is proven
and give instead of gain.

I want forgiveness when I'm sorry.
I want forgetfulness to wrongs I've done.
I want salvation, grace, and mercy,
and eternal life with God's own Son!

I want to know Christ and the power of his
resurrection and the fellowship of sharing
in his sufferings, becoming like him in his death ...
Philippians 3:10

I WANT TO PEEK AT HEAVEN

I want to peek at Heaven
if I could just peel back the sky
and glimpse at its vast beauty, most stunning to the eye.

I'd want to see its beauty
knowing one day it'll be my home.
See Jesus in all His glory and see God upon His throne.

I would see all of my loved ones,
perhaps even a pet or two.
We would rejoice at our reunion and rekindle the love we knew.

I would glimpse at my inheritance;
the place of everlasting life.
There would be no tears or crying, no stress or days of strife.

I would see the angels singing,
perhaps join them as they sing.
My heart would burst with pleasure shouting praises to the King.

I would see golden streets of glory;
each one would gleam and shine.
See Heaven in all its splendor. Oh, that future home of mine!

If I could peek at Heaven
by peeling back the sky,
I would reach right up and do so, not wait until I die!

*After this I looked, and there before me was a door
standing open in heaven. And the voice I had first heard
speaking to me like a trumpet said, "Come up here, and I will
show you what must take place after this."*
Revelation 4:1

IF I COULD LIVE LIFE OVER AGAIN

If I could live life over again,
I would worry less each day.
I would sing and dance a whole lot more and leave more time to pray.

If I could live life over again,
I would wash more weary feet.
I'd wipe away another's tears, and I'd listen more than I'd speak.

If I could live life over again,
I would ease a tired brow
by spending more time serving others while asking God to show me how.

If I could live life over again,
I'd feed the hungry, help the poor.
I would take and receive a whole lot less and give a whole lot more.

If I could live life over again,
I would trust more and argue less.
I'd be more open and forgiving, and more love I would express.

I really would spend more time barefoot
walking in the grass and sand;
sing louder in the shower and on more issues take a stand.

If I could live life over again,
I would read more of God's Word.
I'd memorize more Scripture to be shared and truly heard.

But life can't be lived over again.
We can only live it once.
No matter how we live it; no matter our needs or wants.

We should enjoy the days given to us;
make the best of life each day.
To be the best in serving God as we seek His chosen way.

He seldom reflects on the days of his life,
because God keeps him occupied with gladness of heart.
Ecclesiastes 5:20

IF I STAY QUIET

If I stay quiet,
I know I will hear
the flutter of angel wings next to my ear.
I'll hear their whispers
and the praises they sing,
and feel their love for our Father and King.

If I stay quiet,
I'll hear creatures abound
and know on the Earth God's beauty is found.
I will hear the wind rustle
through all of the trees
and feel God's caress in a soft, gentle breeze.

If I stay quiet,
I'll feel my heart beat
and know that the miracle of life is complete.
We are wonderfully created
and our life does pulse on
to the strong, steady, beat of God's beautiful song.

If I stay quiet,
I'll sense dependence on Him
and know that I'm human, falling short in my sin.
But I know that His grace
is sufficient for me,
and I thank Him each day for setting me free.

If I stay quiet,
I'll hear a sweet song
that lingers within me all the day long.
I'll feel the desire
to read God's Living Word
and know that each one of my prayers will be heard.

If I stay quiet,
I will sense God's deep love
that descends on my Spirit from Heaven above.
It will surely encompass
the space that I fill;
I will sense His dear presence if I stay quiet and still.

Make it your ambition to lead a quiet life...
1 Thessalonians 4:11

IF IT WEREN'T FOR FORGIVENESS

If it weren't for forgiveness - where would we be?
No need for salvation - no Heaven to see?

If it weren't for forgiveness - how would we cope?
No forgiveness of sins - no life-changing hope?

If it weren't for forgiveness - frustrations would grow
with no outlet for anger or resentments to go.

If it weren't for forgiveness - would sorry exist?
Would we work out our differences with only our fist?

If it weren't for forgiveness - would we even really care
of the feelings we've hurt and the hate that we bear?

If it weren't for forgiveness - would true love abound?
For love's always sweeter when forgiveness is found.

If it weren't for forgiveness - real love would not grow;
for often the "sorrys" are the seeds that we sow.

If it weren't for forgiveness - would we forever be lost?
Would Christ come to Earth - paying the cost?

If it weren't for forgiveness - would we die in our sin?
Our soul in the grave - decaying therein?

For forgiveness is truly what God had in place
when He sent Christ to Earth bringing mercy and grace.

For no greater forgiveness could God give to man
than Christ's death on the cross - with forgiveness His plan!

"For if you forgive men when they sin against you,
your heavenly Father will also forgive you.
Matthew 6:14

IF THE EARTH COULD SPEAK

"I am the Earth: I am perfect and round;
God's bountiful beauty in me can be found.
God did create me with other planets in space,
but I am more special; holding God's human race.
I circle the sun and dance with the stars,
and among all the planets - more popular than Mars.
I am most beautiful with treasures that abound,
while other planets are dark - no beauty to be found.
I have mountains and plants and flowers and trees
and rivers and waterfalls, lakesides and seas.
There are insects and birds and gemstones galore;
every kind of fresh food, and, oh, so much more.
I am your world, much beauty to see,
but mankind does not always take good care of me.
So much has happened - I'm growing weary and old,
and times are a-changing as prophecy foretold.
Yes, I am the Earth in God's vast outer space,
but change is soon coming and I'll be replaced.
One day a new Kingdom for God there will be ...
A new Earth has been promised that will replace me!"

*But in keeping with his promise we are looking forward to a
new heaven and a new earth, the home of righteousness.*
2 Peter 3:13

IF WE COULD SEE THROUGH GOD'S EYES

If we could see through God's eyes,
what would we really see?
Would we see the way things really are or the way they ought to be?

If we could see through God's eyes,
we would look down through the years
and see the heartbreak of broken dreams; all the sorrows and the tears.

If we could see through God's eyes,
tears would surely flow down our face
in sorrow for the plight of man and the need for God's sweet grace.

If we could see through God's eyes,
we would see the sins of man
and wonder why we're not seeking Him and the Father's redemption plan.

If we could see through God's eyes,
we would see unrest and war.
We would see the hate and discontent, and all we're fighting for.

If we could see through God's eyes,
we would see the justice done
for those that need defending and life's battles that are won.

If we could see through God's eyes,
we'd also see what is right
within the world He's created and seek Him with all our might.

If we could see through God's eyes,
we'd see joy, laughter, tears
in the celebration of new life and the passing of the years.

If we could see through God's eyes
we would laugh at all the things
that humor adds to all our lives and the joy that laughter brings.

Yes, if we could see through God's eyes,
we'd see things differently.
We'd look beyond our narrow lives to see what He would see.

For the eyes of the Lord range throughout the earth
to strengthen those whose hearts are fully committed to him.
2 Chronicles 16:9

I'LL TAKE A STAND

I'll take a stand if I have to.
You know, Lord this is true.
For someone's got to do so
though those willing may be few.

I'll take a stand if I have to
for someone in the right
who has been wronged by injustice.
Yes, for them, I'll stand and fight.

I'll take a stand if I have to
against the bullies of this world
who think they're better and tougher
when their meanness is unfurled.

I'll take a stand if I have to
for those from other lands
who see freedom in this country
from their nation's harsh demands.

I'll take a stand if I have to
as I go about my day
and hope that stance is reflected
in what I do and say.

I know you took a stand, dear Lord,
when you came to Earth to die.
You willingly stood up for our sins;
our salvation you did buy.

So, help us take a stand, dear Lord,
give us a guiding hand
to take on what we know is right
Yes, help us take a stand!

Therefore, put on the full armor of God,
so that when the day of evil comes, you may be able to stand your ground,
and after you have done everything, to stand.
Ephesians 6:13

I'M COMING BACK

"I'm coming back, said Jesus,
I'm returning to Earth one day.
Just listen and fully trust Me,
and believe in what I say."

"I'm coming back, said Jesus,
knowing not the day or time,
but I will return again this way
to claim all who are mine."

"I'm coming back, said Jesus,
I won't leave you forsaken and alone.
I'm leaving you the Holy Spirit,
who will safely lead you home."

"I'm coming back, said Jesus,
The proof is in the grave.
The stone rolled back, I rose again,
through My death, you I did save."

"My folded burial cloth, not crumpled;
reflecting coming back - not done.
My mission is not finished
until each chosen soul is won."

"I'm coming back, said Jesus,
all you must do is believe.
In so doing, you can surely know,
eternal life you will receive."

"I'm coming back, said Jesus,
just hold on to what I say.
I'll never leave you nor forsake you;
I will come back again one day."

*"For as the lightning comes from the east and flashes to the west,
so will be the coming of the Son of Man."*
Matthew 24:27

IN THIS PLACE

In this place is a quiet soul
content within the Lord;
a calming stillness lingers there in accordance with His Word.

In this place is a happy heart
lifting praise unto the King;
overflowing with songs of gladness. You can hear the angels sing.

In this place is a holy house
wherein God's Spirit lives;
the Holy Ghost resides within; God's testament it gives.

In this place is a house of prayer
lifting praise to God above;
a place where one can clearly see the temple of His love.

This human shell is God's dwelling
regardless of status or race;
treat it with respect and honor, for His spirit lives in this place.

Do you not know that your body is a temple of the Holy Spirit,
who is in you, whom you have received from God?
1 Corinthians 6:19

IN YOU MY HEART BELONGS

When I stand before you, Jesus,
and confess to you my sins,
I know I'll be accountable
before new life begins.

You'll lovingly sit me by your throne
and question all I've done;
discuss my worries, doubts, and fears,
and what I did for you, God's Son.

You'll tenderly reprimand me
for the choices that I made,
for my sinful indiscretions,
and the times that I had strayed.

We'll discuss not leaning more on you
nor trusting in your way;
not careful with my actions
nor the words that I would say.

We'd talk about love and laughter,
and the Scripture I'd embrace;
how I shared with others your mighty love,
and your mercy and saving grace.

And I know when we're done talking
and you send me beyond Heaven's Gate,
that regardless of my actions,
it was you who sealed my fate.

For your willingness to die for me,
for taking on all my wrongs;
your sacrifice is my salvation,
and in you my heart belongs!

*"But I tell you that men will have to give account
on the day of judgment for every careless word they have spoken."*
Matthew 12:36

INTENTIONALLY FLAWED

"Intentionally flawed," reads the tag
on the pair of jeans on the rack.
A rip at the pocket, a tear at the knee,
hems frazzled at the back.

No two pair are exactly alike,
flawed purposely to be unique.
Though we know they are new, never been worn,
its perfection, with the flaws, that we seek.

We can compare ourselves to that pair of jeans;
flawed intentionally for all to see.
For God designed us just that way,
Knowing, with flaws, what we can be.

We're perfect in the Master's eyes;
our flaws His grand design.
We're each unique in our own special way.
No two alike we'll find.

We often strive for perfection
in the life we try to lead;
often getting most frustrated
in thinking perfection is what we need.

But our flaws are what make us special,
God designed us each this way.
Appreciate those imperfections.
God's creation is on display!

*"Before I formed you in the womb I knew you,
before you were born I set you apart ..."*
Jeremiah 1:5

IT'S ALL ABOUT JESUS

When you wake in the morning and thank God for
the day, and trust He will walk beside you,
remember it's all about Jesus.
He'll be with you in all that you do.

When you breathe in and out, heart beating steady and
slow, when life's pulse just keeps throbbing along,
remember it's all about Jesus.
You'll march to the beat of His song.

When someone is rude and your feelings are hurt,
and your emotions have all gone awry,
remember it's all about Jesus.
When tears fall He is there when you cry.

Sometimes you'll be up, sometimes you'll be down,
oftentimes you'll lose or you'll win.
Remember it's all about Jesus.
He will see you through life's thick and thin.

When you've lost your job and the bills pile up, and
you worry where you'll get your next meal,
remember it's all about Jesus.
He'll help see you through this ordeal.

When a loved one passes on and you feel all alone,
and life just does not seem the same,
remember it's all about Jesus.
It's for you, to this Earth, that He came.

When slander has been spoken, racial slurs have been
said, and prejudicial attitudes abound,
remember it's all about Jesus.
Peace and unity, through Him, can be found.

When you fall on your knees crying out to the
Lord, begging Him to forgive you of sin,
remember it's all about Jesus.
His sacrifice allowed salvation to begin.

When you lie down at night at the end of the day,
and you thank God for all things given you,
remember it's all about Jesus.
His love is everlasting and true!

*Let us fix our eyes on Jesus, the author and perfecter of our faith,
who for the joy set before him endured the cross, scorning its shame,
and sat down at the right hand of the throne of God.*
Hebrews 12:2

IT'S NOT "GOODBYE"

I do not like to say "goodbye"
to friends along the way,
but rather "see you later"
is what I'd really want to say.

My leaving's part of the journey,
and our paths may cross again.
We may not know the time or place,
or even if there is a "when."

But you'll always remain with me.
We'll never be far apart.
I'll just have to stop and think of you,
for I hold you in my heart.

So, do not see this as "goodbye",
for what I'd really rather say
is "see you later" in this life,
and for each of you I'll pray.

That even if our paths not cross,
I know you'll understand.
I have prayed to the Heavenly Father
that He keep you in His Hand.

"See, I have engraved you on the palms of my hands ..."
Isaiah 49:16

IT WASN'T THE NAILS

It wasn't the nails that held Him fast
to the cross upon the hill.
It was His love for all mankind
and to do His Father's will.

It wasn't the nails that held Him fast
after dragging the cross to its place.
It was the knowledge of what it meant
to save the human race.

It wasn't the nails that held Him fast
when dying between two men.
With one asking for forgiveness
and the other to be condemned.

It wasn't the nails that held Him fast
when angels could have saved His plight.
His mission was to fulfill this goal;
God and man, through Him, unite.

It wasn't the nails that held Him fast
when the Earth shook and the curtain tore in two.
His whole purpose in coming to this Earth
was to suffer this moment for you.

It wasn't the nails that held Him fast
with tears coursing down His face.
It was His deep love and compassion for all,
and His gift of salvation and grace!

This man was handed over to you by God's set purpose and foreknowledge;
and you, with the help of wicked men,
put him to death by nailing him to the cross.
Acts 2:23

JESUS LEAVING FOR HEAVEN

(Words to His Disciples)

"I looked out at My children as the clouds gathered in the sky;
I'm leaving now for Heaven and it's time to say 'goodbye.'

There stands Matthew, Mark, Luke, and John, all faithful to the end;
the other disciples are with Me too, preparing to go where I will send.

Surely, I will be with you always and will see you all again one day;
I've taught you all I have commanded and have shown you each the way.

Your trials may not be easy and your paths may seem uphill,
but I'll always be right beside you in your mission to fulfill.

The way of true salvation you have rightfully found in Me;
My heart bursts with pride and pleasure that you've found salvation's key.

I'm going now to the Father to a place He's planned above;
a place for the worn and weary, and a place of unending love.

I've followed My Father's instructions and My time on Earth is through;
I'm leaving now Earth's journey as I've done all I must do.

And at the final resurrection, I'll return again this way;
just always stay true and faithful, and you'll be with Me one day.

Until then I will be waiting at Heaven's gate with arms open wide;
The Holy Spirit I leave with you and, in Him, you will abide."

*Then Jesus came to them and said, "All authority in heaven and on earth
has been given to me. Therefore go and make disciples of all nations,
baptizing them in the name of the Father and of the Son and of the Holy Spirit,
and teaching them to obey everything I have commanded you.
And surely I will be with you always, to the very end of the age."*
Matthew 28:18-20

JEWELS FROM HEAVEN

Precious jewels rain down from Heaven;
swirled around by angels' wings.
They sparkle in their radiance and pure beauty each one brings.

These jewels are God's blessings;
showered down from Heaven above.
Blessings freely given, reflecting God's mighty love.

One of those jewels is "inner peace";
once captured, dwells within.
It will glow within you always, no matter where you've been.

Another jewel is "mercy";
what a fine jewel this would be.
With it comes forbearance and favor, and compassion for all to see.

Another jewel sparkling
is one of saving "grace,"
reflecting elegance and beauty, and God's pardoning embrace.

And then there's blessed "redemption";
a jewel highly prized.
A gift of redeeming deliverance; Christ's salvation realized.

There is, of course, the jewel of "love";
the most precious gem of all.
This jewel will sparkle the brightest, and its beauty will enthrall.

We'll share this jewel with others,
for its power is profound.
We'll want others to receive it; no greater jewel can be found.

We've been showered with God's blessings;
treasured jewels beyond compare.
Each reflecting God's love for us; each one precious and most rare!

But the fruit of the Spirit is love, joy, peace, patience,
kindness, goodness, faithfulness, gentleness and self control.
Galatians 5:22

JUST THE SAME

Tears from our eyes fall just the same
from sorrows, pain, and strife,
as they do from love and laughter,
and from joys we have in life.

On our knees we kneel just the same
while lifting prayers to Him,
as we do when calling out to God
when our hopes and dreams seem slim.

A happy heart beats just the same
as one that's filled with pain.
It can skip a beat when elated
as it does when under strain.

Dancing feet shuffle just the same
to the beat of a favorite song,
as they shuffle when walking through this life
carrying burdens far too long.

A lump in the throat forms just the same
from the sight of a long-lost friend,
as it does in that one moment
when a beloved life does end.

All our prayers are heard just the same
when uttered on the run,
as they are when said upon our knees
or whispered when life is done.

God's love and grace is just the same
for all of humankind.
It doesn't matter who you are;
it's just the same, you'll find.

Jesus Christ is the same yesterday, today, and tomorrow.
Hebrews 13:8

KNEE-MAIL

I have a message to send to God
but texting just won't do.
And calling Him on my cell phone
would be a challenge too.

I could try to send an e-mail,
but who knows where it would go?
And sending it to Heaven
could be a little slow.

I won't find Him on my "Facebook,"
nor through the "My Space" site.
And I'd confuse the postal workers
attempting to send it overnight.

I could sneak a peak at "YouTube"
to see if He is there,
but that is no way to contact Him
if I want a response to prayer.

God has given us instructions
on which we cannot fail.
It's called seeking Him through quiet prayer
which I'll refer to as "Knee-Mail".

Come, let us bow down in worship,
let us kneel before the Lord our Maker ...
Psalm 95:6

LAUGHTER

He had to outright chuckle when
they struggled on their boat.
The nets were far too heavy,
much more fish than they could tote.

The disciples could be quite funny
if the timing was just right,
would bring laughter to the Son of God;
didn't matter day or night.

The times that they would clamor
for attention in His eyes
to often compete to be the best
and who could change more lives.

Would bring a gentle smile
to His loving, caring face,
and the joy that His disciples brought
in their everyday, hectic pace.

Jesus wants us to have laughter,
as surely He did so;
to think upon good thoughts
and in laughter we will know.

Surely God created laughing
to lighten our daily din.
So, when things seem dark and heavy,
go ahead put on a grin.

Jesus is probably right now laughing
at the funny things we do;
sees the humor in our living
for He wishes this for you.

There are times we must be serious
when tears will cloud our eyes,
but there's also time for laughter;
for in laughter sorrow dies.

Our mouths are filled with laughter, our tongues with songs of joy.
Then it was said among the nations, "The Lord has done great things for them."
Psalm 126:2

LEAD ME ON

Lead me on, Lord, lead me on,
show the way, take my hand.
Help me daily when I falter;
hold me up, help me stand.

Lead me on, Lord, lead me on,
to the place I need to be;
through life's tests, through life's trials,
during my prayers on bended knee.

Lead me on, Lord, lead me on,
through life's darkest valleys low.
In fading light and shifting shadows,
hold me close, please don't let go.

Lead me on, Lord, lead me on,
to the highest mountain peak.
Draw me ever nearer to you
on the climb though I grow weak.

Lead me on, Lord, lead me on,
let me be your eyes and ears.
See and hear the needs of others;
help me soothe, relieve their fears.

Lead me on, Lord, lead me on;
help me be your hands and feet;
carrying burdens for those that stumble,
sharing love to all I meet.

Lead me on, Lord, lead me on;
guide and help me be my best.
Lead me toward the throne of Heaven
'til the day I'm laid to rest.

Since you are my rock and my fortress,
for the sake of your name lead and guide me.
Psalm 31:3

LENT

Lent is a time of things given up,
perhaps even giving in;
drawing closer to our Heavenly Father
and relying more on Him.

It's a time of fasting and thinking through
all the things that God has done;
to help us in this life on Earth
through the giving of His only Son.

It's a time to contemplate our path
in our daily walk through life.
A time to forsake all the daily things
that cause discontent and strife.

It's a time of deep soul searching
of all the ways to be our best;
of giving up our selfish wants and needs,
and, through Him, finding peace and rest.

Hold fast to the hand of Jesus;
read God's Word each and every day.
Lent Season will then have provided
a time to surrender and obey!

*He is the atoning sacrifice for our sins, and not only for ours
but also for the sins of the whole world.*
1 John 2:2

LET US CLAP IN ADORATION

The leaves clap in adoration
to the mighty God above;
their rhythm driven by the wind
and their motion by God's love.

The flower unfurls its beauty
as it opens up in spring;
it's dressed in all its glory,
giving praise to God our King.

The birds begin their chirping
in the early morning's dawn,
lifting praises to the heavens,
proclaiming God's glory in their song.

The sun breaks over the horizon,
sending rays throughout the sky;
bringing light out of the darkness,
God's gift for you and I.

There is beauty all around us;
we must listen and be still.
We'll then witness the unfolding
of His love and gracious will.

Don't let worries, grief, and illness
cloud the beauty of each day.
Let God's blessings chase the shadows
from our path along the way.

Let us clap in adoration
to the mighty God above;
our rhythm by the Spirit
and our motion by God's love!

You will go out in joy and be led forth in peace;
the mountains and hills will burst into song before you,
and all the trees of the field will clap their hands.
Isaiah 55:12

LIFE

(Somehow We Endure)

Love gained and lost;
        not always knowing.
                Heart swells and heart breaks,
                        sometimes not really sure.

Lives touched – moving forward;
        affection can be there.
                Sometimes there is pain,
                        somehow we endure.

Life changes – sometimes lonely
        with people all around.
                At times alone and all quiet;
                        true peace can be found.

Passion within;
        can its fire be stilled?

                In the heat of one moment,
                        it burns in the soul.

                In that one moment,
                        do you hold on or let go?

Respect is an option;
        it often is earned.
                Can be gained, perhaps lost;
                        then again can be found.

Life is a mystery.
        Choices made, right or wrong.
                Freedom of choice;
                        choices not always sound.

Sometimes not really sure.
        Somehow we endure.

Make it your ambition to lead a quiet life …
1 Thessalonians 4:11

LIFE'S FLIGHT

I'm coming in for a landing;
all had better clear the way.
The tower has given clearance with instructions to obey.

I'm holding the course as given;
my path, as mapped, is clear.
I'm traveling with a purpose, and I'm progressing without fear.

My wheels have now been lowered;
the runway lights are on.
I'm gliding toward the landing; many traveled miles are gone.

Life is like a busy airstrip;
people come and people go.
Some charging forth with power; others taking this life slow.

As we daily make life's journey,
there are angels beneath our wings.
The Holy Spirit giving power; fully fueled with what life brings.

Christ is our controlling tower
making sure we are in sight.
Guiding all who seek Him with the guidance of His light.

Many may join us on our journey
or a solo flight we'll take.
But no matter how we travel, God will not, our lives, forsake.

When we come in for a landing,
be assured our path is clear.
For God has traveled with us casting out all doubt and fear!

"The Lord himself goes before you and will be with you;
he will never leave you nor forsake you.
Do not be afraid; do not be discouraged."
Deuteronomy 31:8

LIFE'S PAIN

I've got a pain in my head today
with thoughts all jumbled around.
I think a headache is coming on,
a migraine may be found.

I wanted to make a good impact,
but negative thoughts got in the way.
The head pain is slowly increasing;
I must be careful in what I say.

I must quickly get to the Bible
to change my thoughts within
before I'm overtaken
with life's worries, fears, and sin.

Life really shouldn't be so painful,
nor our thoughts so out of control.
If we'd place our mind on the right things,
searching God's Word should be our goal.

The pain in my head's getting better;
only good thoughts now abound.
I've taken time to read the Bible
where peace and goodness can be found.

Finally, brothers, whatever is true, whatever is noble, whatever is right,
whatever is pure, whatever is lovely, whatever is admirable -
if anything is excellent or praiseworthy -
think about such things.
Philippians 4:8

LIFE'S RHYTHMS

Life is full of rhythm - its pulse moves us along.
Sometimes it's slow and steady;
other times it's quick and strong.

There's rhythm in the timing of our minutes, hours, days;
in the cycle of the full moon
and the sun's bright, morning rays.

It's in the ever ebb and flow of the ocean on the shore,
in the rotation of the planets
within the universe we explore.

There's the tempo of a favorite song with the drums that a drummer plays;
in the movements of a dancer
and the beauty it portrays.

It may be in the banging of a shutter in the wind,
in the steady rhythm of the rain
or laughter with a friend.

It could be in the cadence of the marching of a band,
or in the march of soldiers
when there's war upon the land.

There's rhythm in adrenaline when jogging a steady pace;
the heavy breathing in and out
after competing in a race.

Perhaps the clanging of a bell or leaves clapping in the breeze,
or the waltz between two lovers.
It could be any one of these.

There's rhythm in our heartbeat - God created life this way.
Let the Spirit ever guide us
through life's rhythms every day!

The moon marks off the seasons,
and the sun knows when to go down.
Psalm 104:19

LIFE'S TESTS

What do you want of me, dear Lord,
of life's tests I take and fail?
I try so hard to measure up,
but end up weak and frail.

I'll always be a sinner, Lord,
though I give my heart and soul.
I fail time and time again,
but my intentions you do know.

Lead me to the cross, dear Lord;
help me place my trust in Thee.
Help me give up all that I hold dear
if that's the test you have of me.

As I fall down on my knees, dear Lord,
giving you my love and praise.
I may not know what you want of me,
but I'll trust you all my days.

Through life's many tests, Lord, lead me.
Yes, guide me to Thy throne.
Help me surrender all to you;
knowing none of it I own.

I may not fully understand
life's tests that come my way.
Help me through each test and trial of life
as you guide me through each day!

Consider it pure joy, my brothers,
whenever you face trials of many kinds,
because you know that the testing of your faith develops perseverance.
James 1:2-3

LIKE AN EVERGREEN

The evergreen stands stately no matter where it grows.
Its beauty is everlasting - in its regal stance it shows.

It certainly enhances the beauty of the other trees around.
Reds, and greens, and yellows - flaming beauty does abound.

Without that touch of evergreen, the others wouldn't seem so bright.
It brings out the best in the other trees - yet,
alone, beautiful in winter's light.

Let us be like the stately evergreen. Our
Christian faith both strong and pure.
Our regal stance will be noticed - deeply rooted, our commitment sure.

Our beauty will certainly enhance others when
we're standing among the crowd.
Our touch of evergreen beauty - never fading, standing proud.

The efforts of all others when they're trying hard to please
will shine forth even brighter when we're standing among these.

When we are feeling lonely during "winter" times of life,
remember we're the evergreen - even during times of strife.

We are standing tall and regal among others in full array.
Our Christian love everlasting - our faith is there to stay.

*So then, just as you received Christ Jesus as Lord,
continue to live in him, rooted and built up in him,
strengthened in the faith as you were taught,
and overflowing with thankfulness.*
Colossians 2:6-7

LIVING WATER

Living water flowing
through the landscape of our soul;
sometimes we can feel the power of its steady, constant flow.

At other times, it trickles
and we hardly know it's there,
as we thirst for living water and we cry out in despair.

But when our soul is thirsty
and we long for sweet relief,
we know it will start flowing from the fountain of belief.

Jesus says, "Believe in Me,"
as He pours out all His love,
and from His heart flows rivers of living water from above.

It is flowing from the throne of God
and will surely never end.
Living water will keep on flowing. We will never thirst again!

… Jesus stood and said in a loud voice,
"If a man is thirsty, let him come to me and drink.
Whoever believes in me, as the Scripture has said,
streams of living water will flow from within him."
John 7:38

"Look ahead" should be our life's motto.
Don't look back - it'll only slow you down.
The Bible teaches us this lesson;
in many places it can be found.

God's Word tells us how to win a race.
Run in such a way to get the prize.
You can't do that by looking back;
so, you know where to keep your eyes.

Lot's wife looked back when told not to.
She turned into a pillar of salt.
Looking back on a life most disturbing;
being warned, it was her own fault.

God also told Abraham not to look back;
to move ahead to the Promised Land.
It was a matter of placing His faith in God;
not letting doubts have the upper hand.

Backsliding is a way of looking back;
such a tragic waste of time.
If you'll keep your sight upon Jesus,
your race will not feel like a climb.

Look ahead in both mind and manner.
Don't look back to a past left behind.
Look ahead on life's race placed before you;
a race God strategically designed.

As soon as they had brought them out,
one of them said, "Flee for your lives!
Don't look back, and don't stop anywhere in the plain!
Flee to the mountains or you will be swept away!"
Genesis 19:17

But Lot's wife looked back and she became a pillar of salt.
Genesis 19:26

LOVE THY NEIGHBOR

Love thy neighbor as thyself.
It doesn't matter bad or good.
"Love thy neighbor," Jesus said,
"and you'll be living as you should."

Love thy neighbor as thyself.
Lend a hand when they're in need.
Do not turn and look away
when you're able to clothe and feed.

Love thy neighbor as thyself.
Do not judge the way they live.
Pray for their unspoken needs,
and give what you can give.

Love thy neighbor as thyself.
It doesn't matter their color or race.
It doesn't matter how much they make;
doesn't matter their status or place.

Love thy neighbor as thyself.
Always let them know you care.
Enlighten them with the love of God,
and remember them in prayer.

He answered: " 'Love the Lord your God with all your heart
and with all your soul and with all your strength and with
all your mind'; and, 'Love your neighbor as yourself.'"
Luke 10:27

MAKE THE MOST OF LIFE EACH DAY

If I could live life over again,
I would worry less each day.
I would sing and dance a whole lot more and leave more time to pray.

If I could live life over again,
I would wash more weary feet.
I'd wipe away another's tears, and I'd listen more than I'd speak.

If I could live life over again,
I would ease a tired brow
by spending more time serving others while asking God to show me how.

If I could live life over again,
I'd feed the hungry; help the poor.
I would take and receive a whole lot less, and give a whole lot more.

If I could live life over again,
I would trust more and argue less.
I'd be more open and forgiving, and more love I would express.

I really would spend more time barefoot
walking in the grass and sand.
Sing louder in the shower and on more issues take a stand.

If I could live life over again,
I would read more of God's Word.
I would memorize more Scripture to be shared and truly heard.

But life can't be lived over again,
we can only live it once.
No matter how we live it; no matter our needs or wants.

We should enjoy the days given us;
make the most of life each day.
To be the best in serving God as we seek His chosen way.

Blessed are they who keep his statutes
and seek him with all their heart.
Psalm 119:2

MANY TALENTS, MANY GIFTS

Many talents, many gifts. What's the difference between the two?
Talents you were born with;
gifts are given from God to you.

You may have a talent of singing, perhaps an artistic flair,
or maybe a sense of compassion
when your fellow man needs special care.

Your talent may be dancing in celebration of this life,
or having a loving, listening, ear
when another is sharing troubles and strife.

Perhaps God gave you a gift of wisdom or of leadership for the weak,
a gift of healing or teaching,
or a foreign tongue which you speak.

Perhaps it's a gift of serving and showing mercy to the poor,
or prophesying of the days ahead
and what the future has in store.

Every good and perfect gift given is from our Heavenly Father above,
and each of us have different gifts
given by God's mighty grace and love.

Fan into flame those special gifts that God has given you.
Do not abandon nor neglect those gifts;
cheerfully give and share them too.

We have different gifts, according to the grace given us.
If a man's gift is prophesying, let him use it in proportion to his faith.
If it is serving, let him serve; if it is teaching, let him teach;
if it is encouraging, let him encourage;
if it is contributing to the needs of others, let him give generously;
if it is leadership, let him govern diligently;
if it is showing mercy, let him do it cheerfully.
Romans 12:6-8

MARRIAGE IS....

Marriage is a commitment----
>   a life-time pledge of love,
>   a union of sharing and caring,
>   a vow to God above.

Marriage is a contract----
>   a bond of human souls,
>   a partnership during times of need,
>   a pledge that "oneness" holds.

Marriage is a constant----
>   a reminder of all that's dear,
>   a giving, caring relationship,
>   a joy that's ever near.

Marriage is a condition----
>   a forgiveness of wrongs done,
>   a forgetfulness of hurtful words,
>   a sharing one-on-one.

Marriage is a chorus----
>   a song throughout the years,
>   a tune upon the heartstrings,
>   a melody you can hear.

Marriage is a connection----
>   a loving string of hope,
>   a knot of love entwined,
>   a bond to help you cope.

Don't ever forget that marriage
>   is a gift from God above,
>   a symbol of togetherness,
>   a token of your love.

It's a fragile bond of loving----
>   please handle it with care.
Remember it's the little things
>   that are cherished, priceless, rare.

Let love and faithfulness never leave you;
bind them around your neck, write them on the tablet of your heart.
Proverbs 3:3

MAY I HAVE A WORD, LORD?

May I have a word, Lord?
There's much I want to share.
So much that is upon my heart
knowing you listen and you care.

Can you see my brokenness;
my heart that's split in two?
My aching heart is yearning
for the healing that comes from you.

Can you see my tears, Lord?
Each one wrenched from deep within,
reflecting my inner sadness
for every sorrow and every sin.

Can you see my weakness
and the strength I often lack?
Can you see my inner craving
for the power you can give back?

Can you see the envy
and the longings for what's not mine;
all the procrastinations
when I'm running out of time?

Can you see my every frustration
when not making myself clear?
Can you see my inner anguish
when I've lost what I hold dear?

I know you see all of these things
that I'm sharing with you now.
You've given me grace and mercy,
and forgiveness, yes, somehow.

Thanks for letting me have a word
of all upon my heart to share;
allowing me in your Presence
through the mighty power of prayer.

For the eyes of the Lord are on the righteous
and his ears are attentive to their prayer ...
1 Peter 3:12

MESSAGE IN THE BOTTLE

What's the message in the bottle? Is it peace you're searching for?
Do you find it in companionship? Does it heal a heart that's sore?

Is it a message of serenity? Do the contents stop the pain?
Does it dull the hurts that are deep inside? Does it help you feel sane?

Its substance is a poison with a hold that grabs down deep.
It's not peace that you will find there, nor a message you'll want to keep.

You don't need the golden liquid that often burns on its way down,
nor the pills that dull the senses, where no peace is ever found.

For its grasp is most addictive, a hold you cannot live without.
You'll go to it again and again, for its message of hopelessness and doubt.

Get rid of the substance in the bottle. Find the
message in God's Word instead.
There you will find true hope and love, where
your soul and spirit will be fed.

Grab the Bible, not the bottle. Read His Word to see you through.
Get rid of your addictions, for God is always there for you.

God's Word is far more powerful, read it daily and you'll see,
it is sharper than any two-edged sword; sharper
than any addiction will ever be.

For the word of God is living and active. Sharper than any double-edged
sword, it penetrates even to dividing soul and spirit, joints and
marrow; it judges the thoughts and attitudes of the heart.
Hebrews 4:12

MY ANCHOR

Where is my anchor when life's raging sea happens
that tosses me every which way, to and fro?
And though I hang on, the waves tumble and toss me,
and swell to such heights I can't see where to go.

Winds of anxiety gust with gale force power
that my muscles grow weary from just hanging on.
Fears from life's storms consume body, mind, and spirit,
as I'm cresting each wave holding on 'til strength's gone.

Sometimes feeling my ship's going to be overtaken
by unrelenting waves that batter and pound.
I'm looking for blue skies as the rain keeps on falling,
searching safe harbors where peace can be found.

When the gale force winds lessen, and I'm tired and weary
from the turbulent tossing of life's angry sea,
I fall to my knees on the deck of my vessel
knowing, dear Father, you are always with me.

Thank you for being that stronghold and anchor
that holds me in place through life's chaotic waves.
When storms again gather on this life's horizon,
I'll know you are there and your mighty strength saves!

... we who have fled to take hold of the hope
offered to us may be greatly encouraged.
We have this hope as an anchor for the soul, firm and secure.
Hebrews 6:18-19

MY JOURNEY

God's working with me every day;
I feel it in my soul.
A "work in progress" I am sure, but only He would know.

I always strive to do what's right
though stumbling along the way,
or taking a detour from His path in the things I do and say.

I sometimes need a road map
or a GPS, I know,
to set me back upon the course that God wants me to go.

I know that my life's journey
is laid out as God has planned.
I need to heed the warning signs; hold tightly to His hand.

I cannot let my failures
keep me from forging on,
nor let failed expectations lead me thinking I've done wrong.

I must always seek God's guidance
knowing He walks each step with me,
even when I falter, not seeing what He can see.

He knows that I am human,
and He knows what's in my heart.
He also knows, as I seek Him, I may fail from the start.

But I know that God is with me,
no matter where I may go.
The lessons learned on my journey are surely blessings to my soul.

... let the wise listen and add to their learning,
and let the discerning get guidance - ...
Proverbs 1:5

MY PLEDGE

I am thirsty; my throat is aching.
I'm stumbling in my frantic search.
Not sure how long I can keep on traveling
before I quench this burning thirst.

On my journey, I've become weary;
my feet are dragging along the way.
Often failing; sometimes crawling,
seeking, searching, day by day.

Where is that cool, refreshing water
that my body so desperately needs?
Where's the sustenance I am craving
upon which my body feeds?

It's not water from a well I'm seeking,
but the fountain that flows so free.
The one that springs to life everlasting
that will flow like a river through me.

That life-giving water is from the Savior;
sustaining me to the very end.
He gives this water to all who are seeking,
knowing we'll never thirst again.

Now that I'm no longer thirsty,
I'll summon others to the fountain edge;
to that everlasting, thirst-quenching water.
This will always be my pledge.

*"… but whoever drinks the water that I give him will never thirst.
Indeed, the water I give him will become in him a spring
of water welling up to eternal life."*
John 4:14

MY SHIELD

I'm carrying around my shield today
to ward off arrows of doubt,
but I have faith, and faith's my shield,
no matter what comes about.

My shield is polished and shiny,
brightly gleaming in the sun,
and everyone who knows me
knows my belief in the Holy One.

I'm carrying around my shield today
to ward off arrows of fear,
but I have faith, and faith's my shield,
and I trust that God is near.

My faith may be small and tiny,
but, apparently, that's all I need.
God's Word says I can move mountains
with faith the size of a seed.

I do not fear what comes tomorrow,
for my faith is renewed each day.
My shield is ever ready,
no matter what comes my way.

I'm carrying around my shield today
to ward off arrows of hate,
but I have faith, and faith's my shield.
God will teach me how to relate.

The Lord is my strength and my shield;
my heart trusts in him, and I am helped.
My heart leaps for joy and I will give thanks to him in song.
Psalm 28:7

MY SIN HAS MET THE SAVIOR

My sin has met the Savior
and the Savior has met my sin.
The result is grace in action,
and salvation entered in.

He took my sins and burdens
and carried each one for me
to the cross that was there waiting
for this Man from Galilee.

I can barely seem to fathom
the sacrifice He chose to make
when taking on my every sin
and the price that it would take.

And when I stumble over my sins
that I cannot seem to see,
I'm reminded of the price He paid
when I bow on bended knee.

Asking for forgiveness
that there'll no longer be a trace;
knowing each sin was paid for
through Christ's mercy and amazing grace.

Yes, my sin has met the Savior
and the Savior has met my sin,
and when the two collided,
salvation did begin.

... for you are receiving the goal of your faith,
the salvation of your souls.
1 Peter 1:9

NO EXPECTATIONS

Have you ever had expectations on any given day
only to discover that none had gone your way?

Expecting certain outcomes, not knowing what's in store;
resulting in disappointments, leaving your heart both bruised and sore?

Don't have those expectations on how you think this life should be,
for expectations often falter and can fail miserably.

It's okay to plan and schedule for the days, weeks, years ahead,
but don't let failed anticipation overtake the life you've led.

For life is often easier when you just go with the flow.
Expectations can cause heartbreak and resentment, don't you know?

When you relate to others, expecting behavior a certain way,
you may end up disenchanted in the things they do and say.

Don't expect certain outcomes from situations in your life;
you'll avoid certain heartaches and prevent both stress and strife.

Just know that God is with you. His promise sure and true.
It's not an "expectation" but a "gift" from God to you!

"... And surely I will be with you always, to the very end of the age."
Matthew 28:20

NO GREATER LOVE

How wide is your love, O Lord?
Immeasurable, I am sure.
You demonstrated this with outstretched arms
and the pain you did endure.

How long is your love, O Lord?
Longer than I can truly see.
For you chose to come to Earth as man
and then died on the cross for me.

How high is your love, O Lord?
Higher than the highest stars.
Your love reaches down from the heavens,
and you'll forever bear the scars.

How deep is your love, O Lord?
Deeper than any depth can be.
For the extent of your love is surely beyond
what anyone has given to me.

Your love surpasses knowledge.
Help me grasp this in my mind;
that I be filled to the measure of the fullness of God.
No great love will I find!

... And I pray that you, being rooted and established in love,
may have power, together with all the saints, to grasp
how wide and long and high and deep is the love of Christ,
and to know this love that surpasses knowledge - that you may
be filled to the measure of all the fullness of God.
Ephesians 3:17-19

NOAH'S ARK

"Noah, Noah, build me a boat."
"Build me an ark," said He.
"Construct it high and make it strong;
sturdy enough to ride the sea."

Noah shrugged and looked around.
In this dry and arid heat?
What would people think of this plan?
What would they think of this feat?

He didn't care as he gathered the wood
and all the other supplies.
He slowly began to construct this ship,
putting up with the snide replies.

The people pointed and laughed at him.
Was he expecting some kind of flood?
Even if it rained a day or two,
in this heat, it'd be only mud!

Noah just kept on building,
for God had told him to;
and as he lifted each wooden plank,
he knew what he needed to do.

His family at first were incredulous,
but they soon joined in the fun.
Noah explained God had a plan,
and this job must soon get done.

When the huge boat was finally finished,
they gathered up bedding and hay.
They sought out two of each animal
in prep for the launching day.

When they were almost done loading,
the raindrops began to fall.
They tallied every creature;
accounting for them all.

Noah then closed the hatch and waited.
God was saving this family and man.
The rest of mankind was being destroyed,
except Noah, who followed God's plan.

So, when people point and laugh at you,
listen to God and stay on the mark.
You just might be the only one saved
when instructed to build God an "ark".

"So make yourself an ark ..."
Genesis 6:14

NOT FAR FROM GRACE

I pray that in our failure,
we fail not far from grace;
that God will always be there
with His love and strong embrace.

That He will kneel down beside us
as we bow upon our knees,
praying for strength and guidance;
knowing He hears our prayers and pleas.

In this life we'll struggle,
and each battle will make us strong.
We may be battered and broken,
and our choices may be wrong.

But with God's deep love and mercy,
we'll meet conflicts face to face.
When we struggle with each failure,
we'll know we fail not far from grace!

For it is by grace you have been saved, through faith -
and this not from yourselves, it is the gift of God -
not by works, so that no one can boast.
Ephesians 2:8-9

ON OR OFF YOUR KNEES – JUST PRAY!

It doesn't matter if you're on your knees
when saying your prayers each day.
God just wants to know you are seeking Him,
and it doesn't matter *how* you pray.

You may be sitting at your desk
when you have a request of Him,
or perhaps you have a petition
while working out at the gym.

Perhaps you're in deep sorrow
at the loss of a dear friend,
or depression being your state of mind
when you ask for help to mend.

Maybe you're running errands
or cooking the family meal.
He wants you to converse with Him
and not feel you *have* to kneel.

He doesn't require you on your knees
when sending prayers His way.
You may be standing, walking, or lying down.
On or off your knees – just pray!

Be joyful in hope, patient in affliction,
faithful in prayer.
Romans 12:12

ONE GOD

How many people choose to pray
to a God they do not know?
They wait until disaster strikes
with nowhere else to go.

They quickly fall upon their knees
seeking solace in their prayers;
but do not know to whom they pray,
nor know the God who cares.

It's time for them to realize
in all they say and do,
they must re-direct their chosen path;
take a path that's chose by few.

We shouldn't believe that it's okay
to ignore the God above.
We don't need to live life on our own
when there's a God of love.

Do not wait until heartache comes
when you'll cry out in despair.
There is a God who cares for us;
a God who's always there.

So be one of the chosen few,
and pray to a God you "know."
Don't wait until disaster strikes;
know now in whom to go.

There is one body and one Spirit -
just as you were called to one hope when you were called -
one Lord, one faith, one baptism; one God and Father of all,
who is over all and through all and in all.
Ephesians 4:4-6

OPEN YOUR EYES

Open your eyes and you will see
the homeless on the street,
with no money in their pockets and no shoes upon their feet.
They carry with them daily fears as they wander to and fro,
not knowing where they'll sleep at night, nor tomorrow where they'll go.

Open your eyes and you will see
young mothers trying their best
to feed and clothe their little ones; making ends meet their daily quest.
Their husbands have been deported, sent back from where they came.
They sought freedom in this country, but found hardship, sorrow, pain.

Open your eyes and you will see
many old folks left alone,
with no one seeming to care for them, and their children now all grown.
Their bodies and minds have slowed with age, not moving like they should.
They need to know that someone cares, if only their children would.

Open your eyes and you will see
the addicted and the lost,
who would sell their soul for one more fix; not caring at the cost.
They're always longing and searching; feeling empty deep inside.
They use the alcohol and drugs, assuaging pain they cannot hide.

Open your eyes and you will see
those giving up on life.
They've been abused and have no faith, and pain cuts like a knife.
They search for a higher power, seeking meaning for their soul.
Just getting through another day is their one and only goal.

Open your eyes and you will see
God has a vital plan,
and we must be His hands and feet in helping our fellow man.
We must help each other through this life, whatever challenges there may be,
and know in helping others, we must open our eyes and see!

"For I was hungry and you gave me something to eat,
I was thirsty and you gave me something to drink,
I was a stranger and you invited me in, I needed clothes and you clothed me,
I was sick and you looked after me, I was in prison and you came to visit me."
Matthew 25:35-36

OUR ANCHOR

The Lord is our anchor
who holds us in place
when life tosses to and fro,
when riding the waves
of life's expectations
not knowing which way we will go.

Our anchor is strong
holding us in our place,
not allowing us to drift away.
You know it is there,
safe and secure,
to ride out the stormy sway.

So, hang on for dear life
during storms of your day,
knowing God is your anchor there.
Do not fear the upheavals
that life surely brings,
for your anchor is placed there with care.

We have this hope as an anchor for the soul,
firm and secure.
Hebrews 6:19

OUR DESTINATION

Geese fly in the "V" formation
over plains and mountain peak,
helping others on their journey;
assisting the young and weak.
We, as Christians, should do likewise,
helping others along life's way;
assisting the weak and weary,
and staying with those who stray.
The journey may be dangerous
and the going may be tough;
we may feel we can't go further
when our path is hard and rough.
But if we stay and help each other
toward our goal to reach the end,
when traveling life's lonely passage
with a true and faithful friend,
who will soar the heights right with us
and traverse the stormy skies,
then we'll reach our heavenly destination
and all that Heaven glorifies.
So, like geese in their formation
as we travel through this life,
let us reach out to one another
through our joys and through our strife.
For our destination is Heaven,
and we'll help each one get there;
lifting those in our formation
'til we're safely in God's care!

*... each helps the other
and says to his brother, "Be strong!"*
Isaiah 41:6

OUR JOURNEY

We follow a path, sometimes rocky and rough,
and sometimes there's a fork in the road.
Indecision can stop us as we look right and left;
uncertain of the way we should go.

Knowing what's right, sometimes we choose wrong,
and though faltering, we forge on ahead.
We can only believe that the wrong path we've taken
has a purpose in the life we have led.

Perhaps the wrong paths and wrong choices we make
are the design of God's overall scheme
of the life-plans God made before we were born
and the purpose of our lives He has seen.

We can only trust God in our journey on Earth
that we're fulfilling His plan as designed.
Knowing we're human, and we stumble and falter,
as we search out His plans as defined.

I fervently pray from the depth of my soul
that no matter the path that we choose,
that our journey will reflect His deep mercy and grace,
and His Son, for our wrongs, paid our dues.

*Then they said to him, "Please inquire of God to learn whether
our journey will be successful."*
Judges 18:5

God loves us more than we can know,
that's why He sent his Son;
because we're flawed as a result of sin
and needed sacrifice was done.

God knew sin would play a part
in the lives that we would lead.
And, yes, the flaws are always there,
but God knows our every need.

He loves us more than words can say;
hence, the indescribable gift He gave.
He knew this when He sent his Son
to redeem, and, yes, to save.

But even with our many flaws,
God loves us just the same.
Salvation was His precious plan
and the reason why Jesus came.

Yes, God does love us dearly.
We truly know that this is so.
So, look beyond the many flaws
for, through us, God's love will show.

Thanks be to God for His indescribable gift!
2 Corinthians 9:15

OUR SOUL

In searching deep within my soul to determine right from wrong,
I've asked the Heavenly Father to guide the journey that I'm on.

We are all human in this life with mortal wants and needs,
but we must seek the spiritual food on which our Spirit feeds.

Our soul often longs for wrongful things, even when we know what's right.
And often, like a defiant child, we'll put up a stubborn fight.

But God knows what is deep inside the very core of our soul.
And since He is all-knowing, our choices He will know.

He knows our every inner thought and all the things we've desired.
He knows our anger, pain, and grief, and when our weary souls are tired.

He knows our sinful nature and temptations that rage within.
He knows our many wayward thoughts and knows our every sin.

He also sees the good in us and the good we strive to do;
and He will take our every burden and gently see us through.

He'll never leave or forsake us, and His words will be our guide.
In Him we'll find rest for our souls, and in Him we will abide.

*"Come to me, all you who are weary and burdened, and I will give
you rest. Take my yoke upon you and learn from me, for I am gentle
and humble in heart, and you will find rest for your souls.
For my yoke is easy and my burden is light."*
Matthew 11:28-30

OUR STRIVINGS

(A Prayer)

We strive after your heart, O Lord,
in each and every way.
We try to do what you would want
in our strivings every day.

You instruct us how to live our lives
and how to do your will.
But as Christians we often falter,
though we seek you, even still.

You tell us, Lord, "Come follow Me,
I'll show you to God's Throne.
I came to die upon the cross,
leading you to Heaven's home."

As believers, we can't walk Earth's path
and follow it on our own.
We must walk hand-in-hand with you, O Lord,
knowing we'll never walk alone.

Help us to see you, Jesus,
in our strivings every day.
Help us do your will, dear Father God,
in all we do and say!

*This is a trustworthy saying that deserves full acceptance
(and for this we labor and strive),
that we have put our hope in the living God,
who is the Savior of all men, and especially of those who believe.*
1 Timothy 4:9-10

OUT OF THE BOX

Step out of the box and believe in Christ;
don't stifle your spiritual growth.
Expand your horizons and open your mind
to wisdom and knowledge - God gives both.

Open your mind to possibilities
and the gifts that God can give.
Envision the future and a life with Christ,
and the days with Him you will live.

Forge ahead on the road to a better way
and the riches that can be gained,
by stepping out of the box and believing in Christ,
breaking loose of the sins you are chained.

For wisdom will enter your heart,
and knowledge will be pleasant to your soul.
Proverbs 2:10

OUT OF THE FLESH

Out of the flesh and into the Spirit.
A transformation
of heart, mind, and soul.
A wrinkle in time of a lifetime of living
that will be with you wherever you go.

Exit the past and enter the future.
Giving up reasons
for sin in your life.
Loosening your grasp on the things you thought mattered;
breaking the strong chains that cause stress and strife.

Give up the hatred, impurity, discord,
idolatry, jealousy,
envy and hate.
Replace it with joy, forbearance, and goodness,
love, peace, and kindness with those you relate.

Out of the wilderness, into a rich life.
A life full of gifts
that God freely gives.
No one more powerful than God the Almighty
to help shed our old flesh where the true Spirit lives.

Climb out of the garments of a past life forsaken,
the way of the flesh
through Christ crucified.
God's provision builds faith and a potent reminder
that only through Him will the Spirit reside.

Those who belong to Christ Jesus have crucified the sinful nature
with its passions and desires.
Galatians 5:24

OVER THE NET

What do you use for a safety net
when walking that fine line?
Are you worried that you'll slip and fall
while traversing life's risky climb?

What do you do "over the net?"
What goals do you try to achieve?
What gives you assurance that you'll never fail?
In what "net" do you believe?

Is your "net" a lot of money?
Is it having lots of family and friends?
Is it a solid occupation
in which your main dream depends?

Life holds two important features,
your "goals" and the "net" beneath.
They're both equally important,
and both must be backed by belief.

The first is the goal you carry,
the dream deep within your heart.
The other is the "net" to catch you.
Both must be in place from the start.

The dreams are of your own choosing.
Your activities done "over the net."
And depending upon your actions,
the results will reflect what you get.

Your "net" must be the Lord Jesus,
not money, family, friends, nor careers.
You must know that He'll always be there;
the "net" to catch you and your fears.

So, go out and do the impossible.
Plan large and dream a big dream.
Don't worry about the "net" beneath you,
for your "net" is the Lord Supreme!

You will be secure, because there is hope;
you will look about you and take your rest in safety.
Job 11:18

PATIENCE

We daily need to seek patience,
even though it may seem rather odd.
In our frantic, rushing, get-it-done life,
we must be patient and wait upon God.

We may not know His plans for us,
nor what He wants to use those plans for,
but we really must take time and listen,
and be patient for all that's in store.

If we are not patient in living our lives,
nor taking time to seek God and His will,
we'll miss out on His mighty blessings and grace.
Yes, we need to be patient and still.

So, in clothing ourselves in patience,
as difficult as this seems to be,
we'll know in our frantic get-it-done life,
it is more of God's will we shall see!

Therefore, as God's chosen people, holy and dearly loved,
clothe yourselves with compassion, kindness, humility, gentleness
and patience.
Colossians 3:12

PART OF GOD'S PLANNING

The workings of the hand of God
are a beautiful thing to see.
Occasions in life don't happen by chance.
They're designed how God wants them to be.

You may think it's just coincidence
when things happen as they do,
but it's all in God's fine planning
and all that's in store for you.

It may be for your strengthening
as you struggle throughout the day.
Perhaps making you a stronger person
for all that God has coming your way.

It may be a firm life lesson
or just something God wants you to know.
Perhaps He's trying to direct you
on the path that you now need to go.

Be thankful for all that arises.
Be grateful for the good and the bad.
Know it's all part of God's planning
in the life that He wants you to have.

"For I know the plans I have for you," declares the Lord,
"plans to prosper you and not to harm you,
plans to give you a hope and a future."
Jeremiah 29:11

"PEACE! BE STILL!"

Are you caught adrift upon the shore;
tossed there by the wind?
The tranquil surface of the sea
hiding currents and tides within.

You cannot tell by looking there
the turmoil beneath the sea.
Lying peacefully upon the shore
all seems tranquility.

The disciples met rough waters
when their boat caught stormy wind.
Then Jesus commanded, "Peace! Be still!"
and calmness settled in.

Emotions are much like the sea;
they can be tossed all around.
Below the surface of the skin,
turmoil and stress abound.

You cannot tell by looking there
emotions riding high.
All appears to be peacefulness,
but anxiety there is nigh.

When you're troubled, stressed, and anxious;
emotions tossed to and fro,
the Lord will then say, "Peace! Be still!"
and He'll calm your inner soul.

He got up, rebuked the wind and said to the waves,
"Peace! Be Still!"
Then the wind died down and it was completely calm.
Mark 4:39

PERFECT CALIBRATION

Are we calibrated?
Are we properly checked and primed?
Is our mind, and soul, and body
finely tuned and precisely timed?

We often need to be maintained;
a tune-up occasionally required.
Like a very fine, well-oiled machine,
perfection is desired.

Our bodies often get abused;
our minds get overtaxed.
With all the stresses in this life
both get way over "maxed."

We must take caution and calibrate;
get the needed rest and care
to handle the many functions
and the burdens we must bear.

The perfect mechanic you will find
is Jesus Christ our Lord.
The tune-up that He offers
surely cannot be ignored.

So, take the time for calibration
so that we can be our best.
Take our burdens to the Savior
when we're daily put to the test.

He'll make sure we're calibrated;
make sure we're tuned and primed.
Geared up and running smoothly
in body, soul, and mind!

*Restore to me the joy of your salvation
and grant me a willing spirit, to sustain me.*
Psalm 51:12

PLEASE DON'T GIVE UP ON ME

I may not say the things I should or be what I should be,
but I know, dear Lord, you're always near.
Please don't give up on me.

I may be most judgmental and critical of what I see,
not seeing others as I should.
Please don't give up on me.

Please help my selfish tendencies, help me more a servant be,
reaching out to those in need.
Please don't give up on me.

And when I sin and go off course, and it seems I've strayed from Thee,
you know that I am human, Lord.
Please don't give up on me.

When life's worries weigh me down, and I bow on bended knee,
help me to seek your guidance, Lord.
Please don't give up on me.

Help me walk the narrow path, for your way will set me free,
help me lead others to the cross.
Please don't give up on me.

Help me to seek your mercy and grace; let this daily be my plea.
Always hold me in your loving arms.
Please don't give up on me!

Yet I am poor and needy; may the Lord think of me.
You are my help and my deliverer; O my God, do not delay.
Psalm 40:17

PRAY WITH YOUR EYES WIDE OPEN

Pray with your eyes wide open;
seek those in need today.
Search out the lost and broken;
helping many along the way.

You really can pray while walking
when pleading for those in need.
It doesn't have to be on your knees
when asking God to intercede.

March forth in preaching the gospel;
it will surely come back to you.
The rewards will be incredible.
It's amazing what God can do.

When sharing our Savior's gospel,
you'll receive it back ten-fold;
for God will bless your efforts
in sharing the love you hold.

Pray like you've never prayed before;
seek 'til the lost is found.
Search for those that may be hurting;
pray God's mercy will abound.

Yes, pray with your eyes wide open,
perhaps not on bended knee;
for you can pray while walking
helping the spiritually blind to see.

God will see you boldly marching;
sharing God's mighty love to the weak.
You must pray with your eyes wide open
when searching out those you seek.

*"And when you stand praying, if you hold anything against anyone, forgive him,
so that your Father in heaven may forgive you your sins."*
Mark 11:25

PRECIOUS MOMENTS

There are moments in time that are special
and quiet times when moments are still.
There are moments that bring us deep sorrow
and others when we're doing God's will.

There are moments that bring tears of frustration,
and it seems that nothing goes right.
There are moments of war and terror
when our soldiers must stand up and fight.

There are moments we turn to the Almighty
and ask that He help see us through
this life filled with so many moments
when we need Him in all that we do.

There are moments in time that we capture,
in the words of a poem or a song,
or the paint brush strokes of an artist,
the moments that were here and now gone.

Our lives are filled with precious moments;
bringing smiles or perhaps a few tears.
May we hold them in our hearts like jewels
always treasured as we live out our years!

How precious to me are your thoughts, O God!
How vast is the sum of them!
Psalm 139:17

QUESTIONS TO PONDER

What is a heart without a beat or a touch without a feel?
What is a lock without the key
or a dinner without a meal?

What is joy without any laughter or deep sorrow without any tears?
What's a lonely night without hope for tomorrow
or anxiety without any fears?

What is a flower without any petals or a tree without any leaves?
What is a dance without actual motion
or a faith without solid beliefs?

What is a life without inspiration? What is a dream without setting a goal?
What is a challenge without a contender?
What is a body without any soul?

What is a book without words of wisdom or a fire without any flames?
What is a friend without any trust
or faults without any blames?

What is royalty without a crown or a kingdom without a throne?
What is a purpose without dedication
or affection without love being shown?

What is a choir without any singing or an orchestra without any band?
What is a fight without sides being chosen
or a war without taking a stand?

What is religion without a purpose? What is the
cross without our dear Savior Christ?
What is resurrection without actually dying?
What is salvation without sacrifice?

In life, there are things we think on and ponder;
questions we have and seek answers for.
In seeking understanding, wisdom, and knowledge,
in Christ we will find all of these and much more!

If there is no resurrection of the dead, then not even Christ has been raised.
And if Christ has not been raised, our preaching is useless and so is your faith...
1 Corinthians 15:13-14

QUIET TIME WITH GOD

I know of all the books in my home that I have,
His Word is the lamp and light for my path.
As I read it each day, I know deep inside
that I've changed for the Lord and with Him I abide.

So, take time to read from the Bible each day
and learn of the treasures to be found through God's way.
Know that the Scriptures teach us wrong from right,
proclaiming through the pages His love and His light.

I sit at the table each morning while dark
and open the Bible, the light for my heart;
But before I begin, I pray "Let me see
the things that you want me this day, Lord, to be."

Be with us, Lord, as we start out each day;
please guide our paths and don't let us stray.
Keep us safe from the many dangers outside
and help us remember that you're by our side.

Give us the guidance and wisdom to know
that the way is not smooth and white as new snow.
It's often quite rocky, with mountains to climb,
but we know that, dear Lord, in you we will find …

A friend that is near us, around us, within;
a friend that will carry us and save us from sin.
Give us the wisdom and knowledge to know
that you will help push us along as we go.

Forgive us our sins, Lord, our un-Christian ways,
and help us in telling of your sweet saving grace.
Help us to forgive others as you do with our sin;
I pray all these things in your name, Lord. Amen."

Your word is a lamp to my feet and a light for my path.
Psalm 119:105

Hate is carried on the wind;
evil fills the blackest night.
Christ was near to coming,
but the Father holds back this plight.

The rapture's been predicted;
many think the time is now.
But there are many still unsaved;
more time God must allow.

Mankind has suffered through the years.
Christ came to offer rest.
But thousands still do not believe,
have failed the Savior's test.

He came to offer every man
a path to Heaven's gate,
but they struggle on life's old worn path
not knowing their final fate.

The time is drawing very near.
God's timing is right on key.
He must patiently hold the angels back
before setting them Earth-bound free.

He'll take this moment to reflect,
this time to justify,
the foretold rapture of those on Earth
in the twinkling of an eye.

Christ hears cries drifting in the wind;
evil fills the blackest night,
waiting for the Father's signal
to return through rapture's flight.

"No one knows about that day or hour,
not even the angels in heaven,
nor the Son, but only the Father."
Matthew 24:36

REALITY

People have to face reality,
even in this ever-changing human race.
Some take alcohol and drugs
just because they cannot face
all the changes, all the people, all that's new.
If they only knew the wonders God can do!

They would then change all their ways at once
filled with love, peace, and joy to the brim.
They would shout and sing the wonders of the Lord.
The world would spin while they commune with Him.

And in this sweet communion
they'd forget how grim their soiled lives used to be.
The Holy Trinity awaits beside each man
that each man might, through them, be set free!

*These are a shadow of the things that were to come;
the reality, however, is found in Christ.*
Colossians 2:17

REDEDICATE YOUR LIFE TO JESUS

Rededicate your life to Jesus;
renew the Holy Spirit within.
Praise God for all His blessings;
ask forgiveness of your sin.

Cry the many tears of sorrow;
cleansing sadness from the soul.
Laugh the laughter God intended
to heal and make you whole.

Pray the prayer that should be uttered;
sing the songs that we should sing.
Say the words when someone's listening,
professing Christ, our Savior King.

Worship God the Holy Spirit;
praise Jesus, the Holy Son.
Edify the Holy Spirit -
Holy Trinity – Holy One.

Tell the precious saving story
of Christ who died for you.
Thank the Lord for all His glory;
for His intercession too.

The mighty God in Heaven
is calling judgment from His throne.
Thank the Lord for interceding
from the cross to Heaven's home.

*Therefore he is able to save completely those who come to God
through him, because he always lives to intercede for them.*
Hebrews 7:25

REFINED BY THE MASTER

We've been refined by the Master.
He's held us over the fire.
He knows the right method and timing
in our perfection to acquire.

Like a silversmith, He'll purify us;
make our spirit, like silver, shine.
He'll keep His eye upon us
in this process to refine.

He knows the perfection of silver,
not holding over flames too long.
The perfect timing of our troubles,
like those flames, will make us strong.

He'll know we've been refined and polished
to just the right degree,
for His image will be evident,
His reflection for all to see.

We've been refined by the Master.
He has held us over life's flame.
And like the finest silver,
our perfection He will claim.

"… I will refine them like silver and test them like gold."
Zechariah 13:9

REFLECTED IN THE EYES

What you're truly saying is reflected in your eyes.
Though words may have been spoken,
the meaning's in disguise.

Your eyes may be crying sorrow while you're saying you're just "fine,"
but if no one is really looking,
they won't read between the lines.

Your eyes may reflect pure happiness when there's no smile on your face,
but they'll know while gazing at you
that true joy is in place.

You may look at someone with compassion;
by your gaze they know you care.
No words exchanged or spoken,
just the glance that you did share.

Your eyes may be fierce with anger, though no yelling has been poured out.
But the smoldering embers are burning
behind the fury that your eyes shout.

You may look at someone proudly for the actions they have done.
They'll see the pride reflected there
and the respect that they have won.

Your eyes may speak of pure love and all the affection that you hold
for the person that you cherish,
unspoken words your eyes have told.

Sorrow, joy, compassion; anger, pride, and love,
are all reflected in the eyes, over and above,
the words that are not spoken, no whisper, shout, or call,
no sighs, no sound, no speaking,
for your eyes have said it all.

The commands of the Lord are radiant,
giving light to the eyes.
Psalm 19:8

RELENTLESS

What is more relentless than the passing of the time?
The minute hand keeps spinning, the hourly clock bells chime.

The planets move in rotation, the Sun and Moon slip by,
passing Earth in every cycle, their sequence will not die.

Light appears on the horizon, the sun at dawn will rise.
A new day just beginning, daylight never in disguise.

At dusk that light will lessen, the moon casts its amber glow;
moonbeams casting lengthened shadows, the dusks will come and go.

We can trust God in His timing, our days and years are planned.
He knows our path, our life, our death, each moment held in His hand.

The years will keep on passing, births and deaths will still occur.
Life will keep right on advancing, of this we can be sure.

Through the ages time will change things, but one constant will remain,
God created time for the passing, no circumstance can restrain.

The moon marks off the seasons,
and the sun knows when to go down.
Psalm 104:19

REMEMBERING JESUS

In the quietness of the starry nights as the wind whipped through their hair,
the disciples sought your strength and might.
They knew, Lord, you were there.

Your Spirit was felt upon the wind; your voice upon the breeze.
You left them wisdom and knowledge,
and told them to "think on these."

The day you walked on water was a shock to everyone.
The many miracles you performed
made them wonder at what you'd done.

They pondered the Last Supper, dipping bread and washing feet,
and the love your actions taught them
in saying, "Do in remembrance of Me."

They were convicted by your actions and the vigor you portrayed
when you tossed the money tables
from the temple courts that day.

Thinking back to the quiet garden when you told them, "pray with Me,"
and their regret for not staying awake
in the Garden of Gethsemane.

They were amazed when the rock was rolled from the tomb that you were in.
They fell on their knees in worship
for you indeed had rose again.

They spread the good news far and wide, telling others of your love,
your saving grace and salvation,
and the Holy Spirit from above.

Yes, in the quiet of the starry nights, the wind whipping through their hair,
they gained the strength and might they sought
and knew, Lord, you were there.

*Then Jesus came to them and said, "All authority in heaven and on earth
has been given to me. Therefore go and make disciples of all nations,
baptizing them in the name of the Father and of the Son and of the Holy Spirit,
and teaching them to obey everything I have commanded you.
And surely I will be with you always, to the very end of the age."*
Matthew 28:18-20

RESOLUTIONS

"I'll make a list of resolutions,"
I tell myself each year,
to be a better person
and to which I must adhere.

I plan to lose those extra pounds
and work more on my weight.
I plan to eat more healthy foods
and less "sweets" upon my plate.

I resolve to be more punctual
for all the meetings I must attend;
refer more to my calendar
upon which I should depend.

I'll spend more time building friendships
and give each one a call,
and listen more attentively,
giving each of them my all.

I plan to give more to charity,
to help my fellow man;
to set aside enough funds for this
to do the best I can.

Last, but not least, I'll give to God
my time in praise and prayer;
read His Living Word each day,
His love and salvation share.

I'll make my list and hang it up
where daily I will see
the resolutions I have made
to be a better "me!"

*Do your best to present yourself to God as one approved,
a workman who does not need to be ashamed and who
correctly handles the word of truth.*
2 Timothy 2:15

ROCK BOTTOM

As he raised his hands above his head
crying, "Lord, what have I done?"
the signs of his addictions up and down his life were strung.
There were so many tragic signs
of the life he chose to lead.
Alcohol and drugs were evident in the habits he must feed.

He'd often sit still quietly
trying to focus upon each task,
but soon became frustrated, knowing his habit the drugs would mask.
He would borrow, beg, and steal
just to get another "high;"
not caring that others suffered as they'd sadly ask him "why?"

And when he hits rock bottom
and has fallen on his knees,
asking God to come and help him; help him through his habits "please."
God will surely be there listening,
for He's there each time we pray,
giving strength and motivation if, from Him, we do not stray.

And when he cries out to the Father
for all the wrongs that he has done,
he'll have taken the first step toward healing and will know that he has won
the fight of his addictions,
and in his quest he must take care,
always remembering the solution is on his knees to God in prayer.

Then you will call, and the Lord will answer;
you will cry for help, and he will say: Here am I.
Isaiah 58:9

RUSHING TO THE EDGE

Time rushes to the edge of tomorrow.
Waves rush to the edge of the sea.
Feelings rush to the edge of emotions
and Goals toward reality.

Teardrops rush to the edge of falling.
Fingers rush to the edge of touch.
Footsteps rush to the doorway's threshold.
Living life and expecting much.

Love rushes to the edge of blindness.
"Love is blind" they always say.
Insight rushes to the edge of knowledge
and Intuition toward the right way.

What's "Right" rushes to the edge of faith,
and Faith rushes to God's Throne.
The Pearly Gates on the edge of Heaven
is where God waits to receive His own.

If you find you're always rushing,
stop and take the time to pray
that a sense of peace surrounds you
in your "rushing to the edge" each day!

*I will hasten and not delay
to obey your commands.*
Psalm 119:60

SACRIFICIAL LOVE

It's not a sacrifice unless it hurts
when letting something go,
for it's not a sacrifice if not felt
to the very depths of your soul.
There is no greater pain in life
that cuts so deep and wide;
it swiftly drops you to your knees
leaving scars you cannot hide.
It doesn't matter the sacrifice,
lifestyle, possessions, friend.
A sacrifice is a surrender,
a finality, an "end."
Sometimes there is no other course
when giving up what you love,
and no one knows this better than
our Heavenly Father above.
We do not walk this path alone
when sacrifice must be done,
for the Father walked this painful path
when He gave His Only Son.
He knows the strength, the hurt, the pain
that's there when letting go,
and the surrendering it really takes
for sacrificial love to show.

For God so loved the world that he gave his one and only Son,
that whoever believes in him shall not perish
but have eternal life.
John 3:16

"I'm here to serve," Jesus said, as He knelt upon His knee
washing the feet of the disciples knowing the men they'd come to be.
He gently cleansed their weary feet, advising them to do the same,
as He supped with them that dinner hour glad that each disciple came.

"I'm here to serve," Jesus said, as He walked the dusty road
telling others to walk that extra mile while carrying another's load.
Be a servant and look for ways to help your fellow man,
walk in their shoes, give up your cloak, lift burdens when you can.

"I'm here to serve," Jesus said, as He healed the sick and blind;
healing illness and afflictions, and diseases He would find.
He'd often touch the weary brow, easing pain along the way;
they would see His love in action as He went throughout the day.

"I'm here to serve," Jesus said, as He sat upon the hill
and fed the multitudes fish and bread until they got their fill.
To be a leader one must serve and His service surely showed
as they gathered up the pieces in the baskets that overflowed.

"I'm here to serve," Jesus said, teaching to forgive and forget,
how to love unconditionally, how to give more than to get,
how to recognize injustice, how to turn the other cheek,
how to help the lost and broken, how to understand the meek.

"I'm here to serve," Jesus said, as He hung upon the tree,
this King of kings, Lord of lords, this man from Galilee.
"I've come to lead all people to My Father's throne above."
He did so with grace and mercy, and through sacrificial love.

He was a servant leader, and His message still rings true
that we should serve through our actions in the things we say and do.
Following His example so that others can plainly see
that we follow in Christ's footsteps in how we ought to be.

"For even the Son of Man did not come to be served, but to serve,
and to give His life as a ransom for many."
Mark 10:45

SHIFTING TO SLOW

(Pursuing Jesus)

You're always in a hurry.
What are you trying to catch?
You're always flitting here and there;
a pace no one can match.

You're certainly a busy person,
always on the go.
No time to stop and take a breath;
no time to shift to "slow."

What really are you pursuing,
and where is it taking you?
Is it worth the time and effort
to put your "all" in what you do?

If we'd take this very same effort
in our busy, hectic, day
and pursue the Lord of Heaven
and follow in His way.

Its worth would be much more than
the status you might gain;
the bank accounts, expensive cars,
the high ranking you'd attain.

So, pursue the things that matter,
love of Jesus, family, friends.
Know that you've achieved success
before your life on this Earth ends.

Life would be much more relaxing,
not always on the go.
When taking time to pursue Jesus,
you'll automatically shift to "slow."

My dear brothers, take note of this:
Everyone should be quick to listen, slow to speak
and slow to become angry ...
James 1:19

SIGNS

The sign reads "Yield", but we push ahead
not caring who's in the way.
In our haste to be at the front of the line
we choose to disobey.

The sign reads "One Way" on the road of life
giving directions in the way we should go.
But the quicker path would be the other way,
so, we unwisely go against the flow.

The sign reads "Caution." We must be aware
that we may have to slow down on this path.
It doesn't mean to speed on ahead
causing frustration and possible wrath.

The sign reads "Stop." We must look both ways.
It's dangerous if we move on ahead
without first stopping to make sure the way
is clear on the path we will tread.

God, too, is giving us directional signs
to show us the way through this life.
If we'd only just follow the direction He gives,
we'd avoid lost and uncharted strife.

Take time to follow the many signs given
by our Heavenly Father with love,
who will lead us safely through life on this Earth
to our Heavenly home above!

... for he guards the course of the just
and protects the way of his faithful ones.
Proverbs 2:8

SILENT SPLENDOR

All is quiet in silent splendor.
A hushed stillness in the air.
Though if one should listen closely,
sounds abound from everywhere.

A dog barks in the distance.
A clock ticks the time away.
You can hear birds outside chirping
in the passing of the day.

Not often is one granted
the sweet solitude one seeks
while listening for every moment
when only silence speaks.

It's a time of deep reflection,
perhaps whispering a prayer or two;
a time to ponder the future
and all the goals and dreams of "you."

But know in those tranquil moments
that come far and few between,
to rejoice in the silent splendor
of those moments unforeseen.

Let him sit alone in silence,
for the Lord has laid it on him.
Lamentations 3:28

SOAR ON WINGS LIKE EAGLES

Help us soar on wings like eagles,
daily renewing the strength we need.
You know the challenges of our days, Lord;
You know the flock we tend and feed.

You know the comfort needed daily
striving to bring the "lost" to you,
for we bring good tidings in your name, Lord,
and share with them what they must do.

As our shepherd, please help us, Father,
gather your sheep and keep them near,
leading them to the throne of Heaven,
showing them there should be no fear.

Give us strength when we are tired, Lord;
increase our strength when we are weak.
Bring us hope when hope seems fading;
give us peace for which we seek.

Help us run and not grow weary.
Help us walk and not be faint.
When life's demands can seem most tiresome,
give us power, Lord, without restraint.

Help lift our eyes unto the heavens
knowing always to give you praise.
Show the plans that you have for us.
Keep us near you all our days!

... but those who hope in the Lord will renew their strength.
They will soar on wings like eagles;
they will run and not grow weary, they will walk and not be faint.
Isaiah 40:31

SPREADING GOD'S WORD

Do it now; get it done.
There is no time to waste.
Don't put off until tomorrow
what must now be done in haste.

Daily encourage one another
while it is called "today,"
so that your hearts will not be hardened
by sin's deception along the way.

Today is tomorrow's yesterday;
you cannot recapture what's left undone.
If the task seems too much of a challenge,
remember it really just starts with one.

Be the one who does not procrastinate
in spreading God's Word. Give it your all.
For completion will surely bring satisfaction,
and you'll know you answered God's call.

Do not debate the circumstances,
nor delay what you must do.
Just remember not to put it off further
knowing that "now" begins with you.

Do it now and get it done;
let God, our Father, be your guide.
Do not hold back in spreading God's Word
and in obedience you will abide.

But encourage one another daily,
as long as it is called Today,
so that none of you may be hardened by sin's deceitfulness.
Hebrews 3:13

STAY AWAKE WITH ME

As I walked My final path on Earth,
I asked that they stay awake with Me,
but on returning, they were sleeping
in the Garden of Gethsemane.

My final hour was fast approaching.
I cried out to My Father above.
Anxiety pounding through My veins
in this outward expression of love.

Bowing, I cried out in My anguish,
"Father, if possible, take this pain;
yet I ask your will, not Mine, prevail,"
as fast approaching that hour came.

I knew the trials that were ahead
must be taken by Me on My own …
As the silence of My dear Father
and the sleeping of My friends, had shown.

I gently woke them and said "It's time,"
as the soldiers marched into that place.
I'd resolved to do My Father's will
in saving the whole of human race.

I'd take on your sin, once and for all,
as the temple curtain tore in two,
with a crown of thorns upon My head
firmly nailed to the cross for you.

I gladly came to Earth as man
knowing the wooden cross was My goal.
To live the way that you each must live,
and that My unending love would show.

As you walk your daily path on Earth,
I ask you to stay awake with Me.
When I return, do not be sleeping,
for I'm your path to eternity!

Then he returned to his disciples and found them sleeping.
"Could you men not keep watch with me for one hour?" he asked Peter.
"Watch and pray so that you will not fall into temptation.
The spirit is willing, but the body is weak.
Matthew 26:40-41

STEP BEYOND YOURSELF

Have you gone beyond the fear that seems to hold you back?
Have you stepped out in mighty faith not caring what you may lack?

Sometimes you need to move forward, not fearing what's up ahead;
trusting that you know you are going where God wants you to tread.

It has nothing to do with geography or a "place" you're heading to.
Perhaps it's a mission or experience, a place where God needs you.

The journey will not cost you money, it will not cost you a dime.
It's a journey of going beyond yourself, it will only cost you time.

Like a sign within a terminal that tells you "You are Here,"
you need to know right where you are, to go forward without fear.

To begin the journey of going beyond, step out beyond yourself;
live a simple life, not a deluded one, in trying to make a name for oneself.

God will provide for the journey as you step beyond today.
Step forth daily with assurance that God will show you the way.

The Lord had said to Abram,
"Leave your country, your people and your father's household
and go to the land I will show you."
Genesis 12:1

STIRRING WATERS

Are you moved to action to help your fellow man?
Perhaps it's the stirring waters by God's Almighty Hand.

Are you seeking more in a life that's gone astray?
Perhaps it's the stirring waters of God showing you the way.

Are you moved to flowing tears when seeing Earth's tragic plight?
Perhaps it's the stirring waters and evidence of God's holy might.

Are you feeling uncomfortable with decisions you have made?
Perhaps it's the stirring waters of the plans that God has laid.

Do you question the laws set by the leaders of your land?
Perhaps it's the stirring waters by Almighty God's loving hand.

Are you losing sleep at night with burdens on your heart?
Perhaps it's the stirring waters, and this is just the start

of a life solely lived for Jesus and all He has to give.
It's the stirring of the waters in how God wants us to live.

You are being called by Jesus for the cleansing of the blood.
It is in the stirring waters. Let that cleansing be a flood!

The Lord will guide you always;
he will satisfy your needs in a sun-scorched land
and will strengthen your frame.
You will be like a well-watered garden,
like a spring whose waters never fail.
Isaiah 58:11

TAKE HOLD

Take hold of God's gift; don't ever let go;
hang on for dear life for you truly don't know
what life will throw at you.
You must be prepared.
Hope is that gift when you're lonely and scared.

Life's trials and troubles will toss us about
like the waves of the ocean, but, in this, we won't doubt
that God's gift is there for us, of this we are sure,
and with hope as our anchor,
we know we'll endure.

Hold on to this gift that God freely provides
and we'll weather each storm
in the flow of life's tides.

... we who have fled to take hold of the hope offered to us may be greatly encouraged.
We have this hope as an anchor for the soul, firm and secure.
Hebrews 6:18-19

TEACH ME YOUR WAY, O LORD

Teach me your way, O Lord;
reveal your truth to me.
Help me not make the same mistakes,
repeating past history.

Give me an undivided heart
that I may fear your Name.
Deliver me from the depths of sin;
your glory I will proclaim.

Hear me, O Lord, and answer me;
hear my prayer this day.
In my troubles, I will call on you,
knowing you will show the way.

Help my faith and keep me strong;
discipline me as need be.
Give me strength and mercy, Lord,
and my errors help me see.

You are a compassionate and gracious God;
abounding in love to all.
Listen to my cry, O Lord;
listen to my call.

Give me a sign of your goodness, Lord;
put my enemies to shame,
for you alone are the Almighty God,
and your love I will proclaim.

Teach me your way, O Lord, and I will walk in your truth;
give me an undivided heart, that I may fear your name.
Psalm 86:11

TEMPTATIONS

Temptation is an ugly beast; it can rear its wretched head.
It calls you to do what you shouldn't do,
and you must fight to do right instead.

It's a struggle with our Spirit, yes, when temptation comes along.
The battle within can be heavy,
and the fight to do right strong.

Is it a temptation to do alcohol or drugs, perhaps an extramarital affair?
Is it to lie and steal and cheat,
or go against what is good and fair?

Temptation is like stepping into a fire. It can burn you on your way in.
There's no good outcome if you follow that path;
just a life of heartache and sin.

Evil is always lurking around to tell you that "wrong" is right.
However, you must take the higher ground.
Take a firm stand and fight.

Remember that our precious Lord and Savior
was also tested with this terrible fate;
He understands our struggles with this
and the heartache it can create.

No matter the size of temptation, lean heavy on what you know is true;
that no matter the situation or circumstance,
you'll know He is right there with you!

No temptation has seized you except what is common to man.
And God is faithful; he will not let you be tempted beyond what you can bear.
But when you are tempted, he will also provide a way out so that
you can stand up under it.
1 Corinthians 10:13

THANKS FOR THE NIGHT

Thank you for the fullest moon
and clearest night.
Thank you for the night-time sounds
and stars so bright.

Thank you for the hooting owls
and chirping bugs.
Thank you for whispered prayers
and goodnight hugs.

Thank you for quiet thoughts
and release from cares.
Thank you for peaceful dreams
and answered prayers.

Thank you for needed rest
and your love so deep.
Thank you for guardian angels
as we sleep.

Help us to awaken
to another day
refreshed for any challenge
that may come our way!

I will praise the Lord, who counsels me;
even at night my heart instructs me.
Psalm 16:7

THE ARMOR OF GOD

Take up the mighty armor of God to ward off evil and sin.
Stand firm in this powerful adornment;
stand your ground for all that's within.

Buckle on your waist the belt of truth, protecting all that is honest and true;
guarding you in every endeavor,
shielding you in all that you do.

Wrap around the breastplate of righteousness
to protect all that is truly good
to safeguard all that is honorable,
defending all that it should.

Put on your feet the gospel of peace, being mindful wherever you go,
that wherever your walk upon this Earth,
peace and unity should be your goal.

Place on your head the helmet of salvation,
protecting both forgiveness and grace;
shielding all that this truly does stand for
knowing you're always within God's embrace.

Hold forth the wonderful sword of the Spirit, the
Word of God is powerful and true.
The Living Word of God is to be protected
for it is active within me and you.

Above all else, take up the shield of faith to
protect us from the swift darts of sin;
to extinguish flaming arrows of evil,
protecting beliefs that we hold within.

Yes, daily put on the full armor of God to withstand the evil of the day.
Dress yourself in this finest adornment,
being clothed in God's mighty array!

Therefore, put on the full armor of God, so that when the day of evil comes,
you may be able to stand your ground, and after you have done everything, to stand.
Stand firm then, with the belt of truth buckled around your waist,
with the breastplate of righteousness in place,
and with your feet fitted with the readiness that comes from the gospel of peace.
In addition to all this, take up the shield of faith,
with which you can extinguish all the flaming arrows of the evil one.
Take the helmet of salvation and the sword of the Spirit,
which is the word of God.
Ephesians 6:13-17

THE ASCENSION

A kiss, a sword, a severed ear,
a look, a miracle, a lonely tear.
The crown, the soldiers, people milling around,
a panic, a departure, no disciple to be found.

An argument, an accusation,
the voices of the crowd.
The sentence, the conviction,
all shouted out loud.

A beating, a thorny crown,
a King's robe of red.
The heavy cross, the bets thrown,
the things left unsaid.

The thunder, the lightning,
the curtain torn in two.
The stillness, the darkness,
the sacrifice for you.

The guilt, the shame,
the tomb with the stone.
The uncertainty, the anxiety,
the fear of the unknown.

Three crosses, two sinners,
a King in between.
A word of forgiveness,
paradise soon to be seen.

The angels, the empty tomb,
the glorious third day.
The whispers, the sightings,
no body, no decay.

The prayer, the promises,
the ascension on high;
the hope, the tomorrow,
the return, eastern sky.

*When he had led them out to the vicinity of Bethany, he lifted up his hands
and blessed them. While he was blessing them,
he left them and was taken up into heaven.*
Luke 24:50-51

THE BATTLE

The heart's always beating, the mind's always thinking,
each strong and resilient in their own right.
A battle is waging between mind and spirit,
and daily there's often an internal fight.

The heart, ever beating, feels warmth and compassion,
and loves with blurred vision that often can't see.
The mind, ever thinking, processes with logic,
only considering how life ought to be.

The mind doesn't care that there's heartache and sorrow;
it doesn't account for the pain that is there.
It only examines the facts of a matter
and often will tell you that life is unfair.

The heart, though, is different, it measures the emotions,
it weighs, with compassion, all that is real.
It knows you can't always measure with logic,
sometimes you must measure life with what you "feel."

The mind tells you one thing, the heart tells you another.
These battling rivals confuse and dismay.
You lean one direction, then change to the other,
and often lose focus on what's the "right" way.

The two surely battle, the mind and the spirit,
causing confusion in what's wrong and what's right.
Sometimes your "gut" feeling is truly the victor
when neither the heart nor the mind win the fight.

But thanks be to God!
He gives us the victory through our Lord Jesus Christ.
1 Corinthians 15:57

THE BATTLEFIELD OF YOUR MIND

What are the weapons of your mind
and the thoughts that rage within?
Does a battle roar beyond control
fighting faith or fighting sin?

What's happening within that battlefield?
Have the troops now stood their ground?
Are they ready to battle for what is right
or lose the victory that could be found?

What are the weapons within your mind?
Are they fear, and lust, and hate?
Are they anger, worry, and helplessness,
a hopelessness of fate?

We can choose the weapons of this battle
and the trenches that are in place.
The weapons of peace, and joy, and hope,
are far better to embrace.

Our artillery should be love and faith;
trust and caring our barricade.
Our stronghold should be the Cross of Christ
and the dear price that He paid.

What are the weapons of your mind
and the thoughts that rage within?
Forge weapons from Christ's deepest love
to battle this war on sin!

What causes fights and quarrels among you?
Don't they come from your desires that battle within you?
James 4:1

THE BEAUTIFUL CUP

The pastor raised the cup high in the air, the most beautiful I'd ever seen.
He asked for a raise of hands of those
who could drink from this beautiful thing.

My hand quickly shot into the air, along with most everyone there.
Who wouldn't drink from this beautiful cup,
its rare beauty beyond compare?

Then, he slowly tipped the cup forward as I'm sure my jaw hit the floor,
for its beauty ended at the golden rim;
inside was dirt and filth galore.

I felt a sudden sadness and pondered what he was trying to prove.
I know that in trying to shock the crowd,
he did so with this move.

He then said people are like this cup, some beautiful beyond compare,
with perfect figures and pearly-white teeth,
classic features and shiny, straight hair.

But over time you can plainly see that their
beauty ends at the layer of their skin.
Like the beautiful cup he holds in his hand,
a beauty that ends at its rim.

Inside is full of resentment and hate, with anguish built up over time.
Anxiety and envy and worry and guilt,
all built up in the body divine.

We need to be careful that filth does not fill
these beautiful vessels God has made.
Our bodies are the temple where the Holy Spirit lives;
guarded carefully, its beauty won't fade.

So, be careful that the evil and filth of this world
do not enter past the layer of your skin.
Let God's inner beauty boldly pour forth,
overflowing the heart's golden rim.

Do you not know that your body is a temple of the Holy Spirit, who is in you,
whom you have received from God? You are not your own; you were bought at a price.
Therefore honor God with your body.
1 Corinthians 6:19-20

THE COST OF A MEAL

(The Last Supper)

You drink the wine and eat the bread,
a most glorious meal divine.
And at the end, what is the price?
Can the real cost be defined?

It really isn't just any meal.
Jesus said, "Do this in remembrance of Me."
It's not a meal you partake of lightly;
there's no monetary cost or fee.

When Jesus was here, the disciples didn't know
why such a meal was being served.
But Jesus fed each one and washed their feet,
though this action was undeserved.

We must remember this sacrificial meal
and serve our fellow man.
Like Jesus, you will be doing God's will,
following God's master plan.

Jesus sacrificed His everything;
He gave to us His all.
He gave to us His very life,
and this meal sends a "call."

To always remember the sacrifice
and the meaning behind this meal;
the giving of His body and His blood,
and His priceless sacrificial ordeal.

After taking the cup, he gave thanks and said, "Take this, divide it among you.
For I tell you I will not drink again of the fruit of the vine until the Kingdom of God
comes." And he took bread, gave thanks and broke it, and gave it to them
saying, "This is my body given for you; do this in remembrance of me."
Luke 22:17-19

THE CROSS THAT YOU BEAR

What is the cross that you must bear?
Is it losing self control
when walking the paths of this life's course;
losing sight of your life's goal?

Are tears falling as you bear your cross
from the heartache and deep pain
of all the things you've left undone
and the things you've said in vain?

Is the cross that you've been dragging
from addiction to drugs and booze?
Is it the loss of inner strength
on a course you know you'll lose?

Are you struggling with the cross you bear
from battling life on your own;
not relying on the strength of others,
nor receiving the love they've shown?

Have you fallen down as you bear your cross;
feeling you've failed in this life's race?
Do you not know Christ died for you
and are "saved" by His saving grace?

Do you shield yourself with that heavy cross;
hiding guilt and shame of your past?
Is it the regret of things you've done
and the shadows that they cast?

You can lighten the burden of that cross;
life's trials can be few,
for Christ has taken on your heavy load
when He died on the cross for you.

He himself bore our sins in his body on the tree,
so that we might die to sins and live for righteousness;
by his wounds you have been healed.
1 Peter 2:24

THE DEPTH OF THE WELL

As you stand by the stones and look over the edge,
and you wonder how deep is the well?
You could stand there all day looking down that deep pit
and its depth you cannot really tell.

Life can be like the depth of a damp and dark well,
never knowing how deep it will go;
not knowing what lies beyond what can't be seen
and a future we surely don't know.

But God, in His infinite wisdom and grace,
will be with us when uncertainty comes
when looking down into the depth of life's well
where the river of grace surely runs.

And when we draw forth God's grace from that well,
seeking solace from the dark and the damp,
we know that regardless of how deep this life goes,
He will surely light that depth with His lamp!

The purposes of a man's heart are deep waters,
but a man of understanding draws them out.
Proverbs 20:5

THE FRAGRANCE OF CHRIST

The fragrance of Christ is wafting
through the air on angels wings.
It matters not your station in life,
it permeates around paupers and kings.

To some its aroma is the smell of death
for those unbelieving and alone;
to others it is the sweet fragrance of life,
leading many to Heaven's great throne.

Let the fragrance of Christ surround your life,
its scent telling others of God's grace.
Its essence will be felt in the presence of you;
its sweetness will reflect in your face.

The fragrance of Christ is wafting
through the air on angels wings.
Enjoy its rich aroma
and the goodness that it brings.

*For we are to God the aroma of Christ among those who are being saved
and those who are perishing. To the one we are the smell of death;
to the other, the fragrance of life. And who is equal to such a task?*
2 Corinthians 2:15-16

THE GIFT OF TIME

Minute by minute, the hours pass;
the gift of time moves on.
We know not what the future holds
as we daily plod along.

What does each moment mean to you?
Do you have enough to spare?
Or are you running on short supply
without a thought or care?

God has given us the gift of time
with written plans on its daily use.
We can spend it doing the best we can
or waste it on careless abuse.

God knows that we live such hectic lives,
not taking time for those in need,
nor heeding His written instructions
for eternal life guaranteed.

The Scriptures are His voice to us,
a beam to guide our way;
a beacon to light our darkest path
in the trials of each day.

Take the time to read God's Scripture
and the knowledge that can be gained,
and know that through this sinful life
each moment God has ordained.

The minutes pass by quickly.
Our time on Earth will end.
Though we know not what the future holds,
on God's Word we can depend.

But you remain the same,
and your years will never end.
Psalm 102:27

THE GREAT COMMISSION

God has special plans for us.
Each one is good and true.
He knows the path that we must take and all that we must do.

He knows at times we may have doubt.
His disciples did, you know.
But He loves us deeply just the same and will lead where we must go.

We may not always measure up
to where we feel we ought to be,
but God looks beyond our failures and sees what we can't see.

He "sees" that in our Christian walk
we strive to do His will,
and knows that even when we fail, there's a mission to fulfill.

We are to share the Great Commission,
as Christ instructed us to do.
All authority has been given Him and commands both me and you.

To make disciples of all nations.
Through people's hearts we must engage.
Sharing that Christ is with us always to the very end of the age.

Then Jesus came to them and said,
"All authority in heaven and on earth has been given to me.
Therefore go and make disciples of all nations, baptizing them
in the name of the Father and of the Son and of the Holy Spirit,
and teaching them to obey everything I have commanded you.
And surely I am with you always, to the very end of the age."
Matthew 28:18-20

THE GREATEST GIFT

I knew I was in Heaven, the throne just up ahead.
I was here to meet my Father
to discuss the life I've led.

The streets were bright and golden, yes, the gates were pearly white;
the angels' robes were flowing
and to see them pure delight.

As I approached the Heavenly Father, contemplating what I'd say
when asked what I'd accomplished
now seemed meager in a way.

Did I feed the poor and hungry? Did I help someone in need?
Did I visit those in prison,
or did I hoard all in my greed?

All the sudden I was trembling as I bowed before His feet.
He placed His Hand upon me,
said was glad "we finally meet."

I felt a little shameful in reviewing all I'd done.
I thanked Him for His gift of Jesus,
His One and Only Son.

He thanked me for accepting Jesus, placing a crown upon my head.
"Well done, my faithful servant,
welcome to eternity," He said.

And then, in a quick moment, I awoke upon my bed
realizing it was just a dream
but must share all that He said.

I must tell of my dream in Heaven, share that Jesus is the key.
The greatest gift to all mankind,
God's gift of eternity!

For God so loved the world that he gave his one and only Son,
that whoever believes in him shall not perish
but have eternal life.
John 3:16

THE GREATEST OF THESE IS LOVE

The greatest emotion on this Earth is the hardest to define.
It's the strongest motivator, and its power can be divine.

The Bible tells us to love our enemies, as well as our fellow man;
to love our neighbor as our self and, with love, do all we can.

But how can true love be controlled when it wants to go its own way?
Its strength can be overpowering, no matter what we do or say.

It can be the sole cause of temptation. It can drive both peace and wars.
It can put to rest old arguments, heal wounds, and open doors.

There is the love between parent and child, a
parent's love enduring, a child's sublime.
There is the love between siblings that can last throughout all time.

There is the love between husband and wife that
should be there throughout their days.
There is the love between two great friends that can manifest in many ways.

Young people must be careful with the love that they seek and find;
for love is a powerful emotion and sometimes that love is blind.

Forbidden love may be the hardest, a love that cannot be controlled.
But God is standing near and knows that love,
and, through Him, His love will enfold.

The greatest love known to man is that of Christ our King.
He loved us so much, He died for us, and salvation that love did bring.

Yes, love is the deepest emotion, ordained by God above,
and of all the emotions out there, the greatest of these is love!

And now these three remain: faith, hope, and love.
But the greatest of these is love.
1 Corinthians 13:13

THE HOMETOWN BOY

This Hometown Boy thinks He's a prophet,
but isn't He Joseph's son?
Just whom does this young man think He is
when He proclaims that He's "the one?"

He claims to be a servant;
preaching good news to the poor,
proclaiming freedom for the prisoners,
restoring sight to the blind and more.

He sits in the synagogue preaching,
"Today the Scriptures are fulfilled;
I state this now in your hearing
so false rumors will be stilled."

He walks the dusty roads and pathways
helping all who are in need.
Helping the sick, the tired, the weak,
and the hungry He will feed.

He captivates His audiences
on every path He takes;
whether inviting children to come to Him
or healing broken hearts that ache.

He seems so very human,
yet He claims to be God's Son,
and the way He lived and died on the cross
proves to all He is "the one."

This young man was a prophet,
though not accepted by those He knew.
We must believe this Nazareth Hometown Boy
came to die on the cross for you!

*All spoke well of Him and were amazed at the gracious words
that came from His lips. "Isn't this Joseph's son?" they asked.*
Luke 4:22

THE LAST SUPPER

Jesus looked around the barren room. The twelve were gathered there.
The meal was planned ahead of time with loving thought and care.

The conversation blotted out the words that Jesus said.
Not all could hear Him as He spoke as He served the wine and bread.

They did not observe His gaze on Judas. For a moment, time stood still.
Unbeknownst to them, this traitor, was planning to deceive and kill.

They did not seem to notice as they took the food to eat
that Jesus rose from where He sat to wash their weary feet.

With towel and basin both in hand, He knelt before each one,
and cleansed the dust from off their feet. This cleansing must be done.

He must perform this humble deed before He left this day.
To leave them love and humility, and to show these men the way.

The supper soon was ending. All disciples had been fed.
They had broke the bread and drank the wine, and Judas had just fled.

He visited with Peter, shared all that he must know;
to be the strength for others on the rough road they must go.

The supper then was over. Each got up and left the room.
None realizing, as Jesus left it, He was walking toward His tomb.

They headed to the Garden. Jesus said He must now pray.
He was thankful for these brethren who had supped with Him this day.

*Then came the day of Unleavened Bread on which
the Passover lamb had to be sacrificed.
Jesus sent Peter and John, saying,
"Go and make preparations for us to eat the Passover."*
Luke 22:7-8

THE LORD IS MY ROCK

We stand on the strength of an immovable rock
in the midst of an uncertain world.
No firmer foundation will ever exist
then the rock of our Savior and Lord.

On that foundation, we will sense divine guidance,
though life's tribulations may frighten us still.
We'll know that the One who sees past, present, future,
will be holding us firmly in the strength of His will.

He will hold us with His infinite love and His mercy,
and show us the way through this life we should take.
He will lead us in the way and let us walk in it,
for He'll lovingly guide us in every turn we should make.

Central to that rock is the deep-seated knowledge
that God so loved the world, He gave us His Son.
The cross on the hill is the beacon that guides us
through this life of uncertainty, knowing "salvation" is won.

He says, "Peace I leave with you, my peace I give to you,
not as the world gives, give I unto you.
Let not your heart be troubled, nor let it be frightened,"
always knowing this rock is lasting and true!

The Lord is my rock, my fortress and my deliverer;
my God is my rock, in whom I take refuge. He is my shield
and the horn of my salvation, my stronghold.
Psalm 18:2

THE NARROW GATE

Where is Heaven? Where is Hell?
Do we really know?
Is Heaven the place for all saved souls?
If we're lost, is Hell where we go?

They say all roads lead to Heaven.
But is that really true?
Can we practice whatever belief we want
and do what we want to do?

Does it really matter that we curse and swear,
and stab our brother in the back?
Does God see the evil that we've done?
Does He know all the good that we lack?

Does it matter that we believe in Jesus?
Does it matter if we don't?
The Bible say it does,
so why do we think it won't?

The Bible says enter through the narrow gate;
don't take the wider road.
For small is the gate that leads to life
and leads straight to Heaven, we're told.

Though the wider road may be more attractive,
and we feel we can travel on our own,
on the narrow road we will have Jesus,
though, less traveled, we'll not be alone.

Our good deeds won't make it easier.
Our righteous acts won't win us a prize.
But Jesus will walk right there with us
and will lead us straight to paradise.

So, follow God's path to eternal life;
make sure you go through the right gate.
Be one of the few on the narrow path.
Start your journey right now and don't wait!

*"Enter through the narrow gate. For wide is the gate and broad is the road
that leads to destruction, and many enter through it.
But small is the gate and narrow the road that leads to life,
and only a few find it."*
Matthew 7:13-14

THE OUTER SHELL

The body is just an outer shell that hides what's deep inside.
You cannot see the inner scars
nor secrets one tries to hide.

Is it a clean and tidy place where the Holy Spirit lives,
or is it a dusty, dirty, home
and despair is what it gives?

Is it a calm and contented house which your actions will reflect,
or is it stress-filled discontent
that others will detect?

It matters not the outer shell. It matters what's deep within.
It's the temple of the Holy Spirit.
Make it not a house of sin.

So, clean up the inner body, no matter if its been marred.
The outer shell matters not
whether perfect or physically scarred.

It may be damaged on the outside or beautiful perfection on display,
but it's what's inside that matters
when you kneel before God to pray.

Do you not know that your body is a temple of the Holy Spirit,
who is in you, whom you have received from God?
You are not your own; you were bought at a price.
Therefore honor God with your body.
1 Corinthians 6:19-20

THE PORTRAIT OF CHRIST

The portrait of Christ was painted
long before He came to Earth;
reflected in Holy Scripture
centuries before His virgin birth.

Redemption was the basic theme
written in the books of old;
leading to the cross of Jesus
and His sacrifice foretold.

The "law" was given through Moses
in the testament of those days,
but "grace" was given by Jesus
to forgive our sinful ways.

The Scriptures are a journey
and a diary of the past
that takes us through the ages
and the portraits that are cast.

Of God's unending love for us
through the Testaments, old and new;
God's Holy Word to guide us
to redemption, sure and true.

For the law was given through Moses;
grace and truth came through Jesus Christ.
John 1:17

THE POWER OF TOUCH

In shaking hands, you're saying
to the person whose hand you shake,
that you are glad to see them and the friendship that you'll make.

When you wipe away another's tears
and listen when they share,
you're reflecting the deepest kindness in showing that you care.

In rubbing someone's shoulders,
massaging their stress away,
you're helping them through their burdens when they've had a weary day.

When you share a kiss with someone,
be it family, lover, friend,
you are giving them a message that only a "kiss" can send.

You can also slap, and hit, and punch,
leaving bruises or a scar.
But when anger surfaces to that point, you've taken "touch" too far.

Touch can have a healing affect.
Don't let violence get in the way
of love we should have for each other and the love we should portray.

No words are needed when we touch,
but the message is loud and clear,
in portraying the love we have inside for the ones that we hold dear.

In hugging someone tightly,
as if you'll never let them go,
is silently saying volumes and through this action it does show.

Christ silently healed with His touch
the blind, the sick, the lame.
He healed our earthly brokenness, hence the reason why He came.

Touching is a silent message,
but its action says so much.
We know that "actions speak louder" and often
better through the power of touch.

When the sun was setting, the people brought to Jesus all who had
various kinds of sickness, and laying his hands on each one, he healed them.
Luke 4:40

THE PRODIGAL SON

The prodigal son lay weeping a hundred miles from home.
He was penniless and homeless; not a thread to call his own.

He was young and quite adventurous; wanted to set out and see the world.
He was tired of being in the same old place; tired
of his many dreams left unfurled.

So, he promptly claimed his inheritance and set out on his way.
He would go and see new places, no longer would he delay.

At first, he had a lot of fun; exciting new places he did see.
There was no where else in all the world right then he'd rather be.

But he quickly found in his travels though that his money just would not last.
He often thought of going back home as he dreamed of his wealthy past.

As he laid there weeping it dawned on him, he
was worse off than his father's staff,
the maids, men-servants, and hired hands, it almost made him laugh.

So, he sat up straight and dried his tears, and soon was on his way.
He'd go home to his father. He'd travel quickly night and day.

His father welcomed him with open arms, for this he was quite surprised.
His father called for the fatted calf, as tears flowed from his eyes.

His brother claimed this wasn't fair. How could his father accept "him" back?
The son who took all and went away when there was nothing he would lack?

God's love is like this father's, for no matter how far we run,
He will forgive and accept us with open arms.
It matters not what we have done.

*Jesus continued: "There was a man who had two sons. The younger one said
to his father, 'Father, give me my share of the estate.' So he divided his property
between them. Not long after that, the younger son got together all he had,
set off for a distant country in wild living."*
Luke 15:11-31

THE RAINBOW

A rainbow stretches north and south,
set there by God above.
"I will not destroy mankind again," He said.
He did this out of love.

He set the bow among the clouds,
a sign to you and me,
and splashed it across the sky above
for all mankind to see.

A covenant from Almighty God;
a vision beyond compare.
The bow is beauty to behold,
suspended, hanging there.

What better frame for God's deep love.
A picture in disguise.
A masterpiece set among the clouds,
God's painting in the skies.

They say a pot of gold waits at the end.
I know the gold for me
is God's deep love for all of us
throughout eternity.

I have set my rainbow in the clouds,
and it will be the sign of the covenant between me and the earth ...
... Never again will the waters become a flood to destroy all life.
Genesis 9:13-15

THE SAME IS THERE FOR YOU

"Come on in," Jesus gestured as I entered Heaven's gate,
"Don't delay a moment longer, you've had a long and weary wait."

I smiled as I took His hand as He quickly lead me in,
and I saw the beauty 'round me, thankful that He'd died for my sin.

I had so many questions, but was it far too late?
Can it get "late" in Heaven? My first question at Heaven's gate.

"No, it's never late in Heaven," He said, "Only laughter, love and light,
and praising, singing, rejoicing; a time where there's no dawn or night."

I almost forgot my questions as we toured this Heavenly realm.
I felt so safe and protected; glad that Jesus was at the helm.

But I finally looked up to His sweet face and asked why I suffered so?
My illness had fully consumed me. I often felt like letting go.

But in my earthly suffering, I tried to not show the pain.
I wanted others to meet and see Jesus, and the life they could obtain.

Jesus lovingly said, "That's why the suffering, so others could see the truth.
Despite your pain and suffering, you were the steadfast proof."

"That though you may suffer greatly in the earthly life you live,
you can still fully depend upon me, know the treasures I will give."

So, now I'm touring Heaven and seeing all He said is true.
If you'll bear through the earthly suffering, the same is surely there for you.

This is the gate of the Lord through which the righteous may enter.
I will give you thanks, for you answered me;
you have become my salvation.
Psalm 118:20-21

THE SAME SOUL

It really is the very same soul of the old man with the cane,
as that of the little dark-haired boy
in the antique photo frame.

The photo reflects a little boy with hopes and dreams and plans;
who has aged and is much older now
with arthritic and wrinkled hands.

It's funny how a life goes by, the years just slip away.
The pages of life turn swiftly,
now that little boy's hair is gray.

Sometimes it's hard to truly believe the passage of time and space,
but the remnants of youth can still be seen
in the old man's weathered face.

God created that beautiful soul with gentle and loving care.
The outward body may wrinkle and gray
but it's the very same soul they share.

Time may weather our body and face, and our
steps may be labored and slow,
but when this life passes and our spirit moves onward,
it will always be the very same soul.

*"Listen to me, O house of Jacob, all you who remain of the house of Israel,
you whom I have upheld since you were conceived, and have carried since your birth.
Even to your old age and gray hairs I am he, I am he who will sustain you.*
Isaiah 46:3-4

THE SANDS OF TIME

The sands of time sift slowly
through the hourglass of life;
each grain a given moment,
some of joy and some of strife.

Each grain receives God's blessing
and a prayer on its descent
that each moment that passes through it
will be moments time well spent.

Do your grains pass through more quickly
than you care for them to go?
Do you plan each one with thought and care,
perhaps wasted they pass too slow?

We should cherish each single grain of time
knowing each passes through only once.
Our life is surely measured
in our sands of days and months.

And as each precious year passes
and our grains of sand grow few,
let us draw comfort in the knowledge
that we did all we could do.

That we spent those years the best we could
with direction from God above.
The sole Master of our hourglass.
The One watching our sand with love.

As our grains have swiftly settled
and the last one trickles down,
we'll know that each grain traveled
are now diamonds in our crown!

"I thought, 'I will die in my own house,
my days as numerous as the grains of sand.'"
Job 29:18

THE SCOPE OF TIME

When God ordained that Christ should come
and die upon the cross,
did He peer down through the scope of time
and weigh how much the cost?

Yes, He weighed the value of such a plan
when He saw both you and me
while gazing through that scope of time
and saw what was to be.

He sent His son, our Savior,
Jesus Christ, our Lord and King.
He saw the sacrificial Lamb
and salvation that He would bring.

He saw that Christ would suffer
at the hands of sinful man;
He knew Christ would be willing
and agreeable to such a plan.

Of dying for each and every soul
if they would just believe
and know the depth of God's great plan
and all it would achieve.

Yes, God did peer through the scope of time
and what He saw was rare.
He saw Jesus dying for all mankind.
No greater love can compare!

This is how we know what love is:
Jesus Christ laid down his life for us.
1 John 3:16

THE SHADOW OF THE CROSS

Shadows can be scary
when cast across our path;
they can stir up doubts and worries
creating fears and inner wrath.

Does evil lurk within those shadows,
in the spots that linger there?
Should we walk within their dimness
without a worry or a care?

Calvary's cross cast a bold shadow
across the hilly ground,
but humanity didn't realize
that salvation could be found,

from the source of that shadow's outline
and the message it represents,
and the meaning behind its image
and the great gift God has sent.

We must look beyond life's shadows
to the light on the other side.
It just might be God's radiance
casting shadows far and wide.

Always walk within Christ's shadow
cast from God's bright light above,
and know that He walks with you
in the radiance of His love.

For the message of the cross is foolishness
to those who are perishing, but to us who are being saved
it is the power of God.
1 Corinthians 1:18

THE SPIRIT WITHIN

When night is dark, the stars are bright,
we don't know why we fear
the loneliness that nighttime brings,
for Christ is always near.

Our bodies are the temple;
the place where God resides.
Through the Holy Spirit within us,
no evil source can hide.

The angels do surround us,
to protect the Spirit within.
No evil can come in or near us.
No worry of outside sin.

The angels whisper softly
to each other as they go
about their daily duties
protecting what they know.

That the precious Holy Spirit
is within each Christian's soul.
Don't fear the night, dear Christians,
for the angels always go

before any situation
that life may send our way.
The Holy Spirit and angels
are within and 'round to stay.

Fear not the dark night's coming,
nor the loneliness that it brings.
Listen softly for the angels.
You might hear their whisperings.

Are not all angels ministering spirits sent to
serve those who will inherit salvation?
Hebrews 1:14

THE THIEF ON THE CROSS

He gazed at the Savior with tears in his eyes
as they hung side by side on the hill.
The Lord had just forgiven all of his sins,
and the turmoil within was now still.
He was a sinner, and Jesus knew this
as they each drew nigh to their grave.
This Christ has forgiven all the wrongs he had done,
and his ebbing life the Lord would now save.
The dying criminal on the other side
would not believe it was true.
But he, who was saved, had seen Jesus at work,
and he knew what this Jesus could do.
Hope and love arose deep in his heart
for this Man who they claimed was a King.
He knew deep within that this Jesus was Lord,
and what this gift of salvation would bring.
It was almost more than he could behold
that he, as a sinner, was saved.
This Christ had just forgiven all of his sins
and saved him from hell's fiery grave.
He truly had thought all eternity lost
when they dragged him to be crucified.
On the walk up the hill, he did not realize
the honor to hang at Christ's side.
Lightning, thunder, and darkness drew near
as he hung there with tears in his eyes
as he gazed at the Man who hung by his side
soon to be with Him in paradise.

Two other men, both criminals were also led out with him to be executed.
Luke 23:32

One of the criminals who hung there hurled insults at Him:
"Aren't you the Christ? Save yourself and us!"
But the other criminal rebuked him. "Don't you fear God," he said,
"since you are under the same sentence? We are punished justly,
for we are getting what our deeds deserve. But this man has done nothing wrong."
Then he said, "Jesus remember me when you come into your kingdom."
Jesus answered him, "I tell you the truth, today you will be with me in paradise."
Luke 23:39-43

THE "TIONS" OF LIFE

Do you give <u>attention</u>
to matters close at hand?
Do you have <u>conviction</u>
when called to take a stand?

Is there <u>fascination</u>
in the light of God's bright flame?
Is there <u>recognition</u>
when He softly calls your name?

Is there <u>motivation</u>
to reach your highest goal?
Is there <u>celebration</u>
when you've reached that high plateau?

Is there <u>validation</u>
to the dreams you have in mind?
Is there <u>dedication</u>
once your dreams have been defined?

Is there <u>inspiration</u>
to do God's will today?
Is there <u>appreciation</u>
for His answers when you pray?

Remember your <u>foundation</u>
is built upon God's rock,
and your Christian <u>reputation</u>
is reflected in your walk.

We must pay more careful attention, therefore,
to what we have heard, so that we do not drift away.
Hebrews 2:1

THE WAY, THE TRUTH, AND THE LIFE

"I am the <u>Way</u>"," said Jesus,
"Walk My path and you will see
you cannot get lost in life's problems
if you place your trust in Me."

"The path may be rough and narrow,
but I'm there each step with you.
If you keep your eyes upon Me,
I will be there to see you through."

"I am the <u>Truth</u>," said Jesus,
"My true testament you'll receive.
When there's no one else to depend on,
you can, in Me, believe."

"For you can rely on My guidance
through all that I've said and done.
I was willing to die on the cross for you
as God's only begotten Son."

"I am the <u>Life</u>," said Jesus,
"You must come to the Father through Me.
I will lift you up and sustain you,
and carry you, if need be."

"I will never leave nor forsake you;
you'll never be abandoned and alone.
But you must believe in My mission
as I lead you straight to God's throne."

"I give you these words of assurance.
Never doubt when experiencing strife.
We'll walk hand-in-hand on this journey,
for I am
"The <u>Way</u>, the <u>Truth</u>, and the <u>Life</u>!"

Jesus answered, "I am the way and the truth and the life.
No one comes to the Father except through me."
John 14:6

THE WOODEN CROSS

As he worked upon the wooden cross on which some man would be hung,
did he realize the suffering
or the praises to be sung?

Did he fathom the great drama that would unfold that day,
the importance of his fashioned cross
and the part that it would play?

He was just a lowly laborer making crosses that would bear
the criminals that were condemned
and the lives that ended there.

Did he realize that Jesus was to hang upon this tree?
Would he have made it better
or perhaps much differently?

Would he have smoothed the pillar, no splinters in the grain?
Would he have made it lighter
for the walk on rough terrain?

We often do not even think of the purpose hidden there,
and had he known it was for Jesus
would have given it more care?

We should strive in all we do each day to carry duty out,
and do the very best we can
and know without a doubt.

That we're doing it for Jesus, for our precious Lord and King.
Remembering in our work and toil,
He blesses everything.

As we daily strive to do His will, unknowing, unaware,
we are sharing God's love with others
in our actions and our care.

*Carrying his own cross, he went out to The Place of the Skull
(which in Aramaic is called Golgotha).
Here they crucified him, and with him two others -
one on each side and Jesus in the middle.*
John 19:17-18

THINK AND BE THANKFUL

Now is the time to be thankful
for all that God has done,
and to reflect upon His blessings,
counting each and every one.

"Think" upon each blessing
that God has sent your way,
and "thank" Him for those blessings
that He gives to you each day.

Don't take God's gifts for granted;
don't push each one aside.
But reflect upon His goodness;
let Him always be your guide.

For great is our mighty Father,
most worthy of our praise.
His greatness none can fathom.
We must thank Him all our days.

God is standing near to bless you.
He has gifts for you in store.
He says, "Ask and I will give to you."
He will give you much, and more.

Say a prayer of thankfulness
always knowing God is near.
Think fully upon God's blessings,
each one sanctioned with love sincere.

Great is the Lord and most worthy of praise;
his greatness no one can fathom.
Psalm 145:3

THROUGH THE VALLEY

When we walk through the valley of the shadow of death,
we know that, dear Father, you're there.
You walk every step in cadence with ours
as you cloak us with love and with care.

It's a desolate place, you know this is true,
as dark shadows descend to the ground.
But we firmly hold on to our faith that you care,
with the knowledge true peace can be found.

And when the night comes, and it's lonely and dark,
and it's hard to see light up ahead,
we know you relate to this same sort of loss
as the night on the cross your Son bled.

We need not feel abandoned, nor solely alone,
on this journey of which we must take.
It's part of the path we must walk in this life;
one which all of us truly must make.

We know others have taken this same lonely road,
and their footprints are ingrained in the sand.
Thanks for assuring us, Father, that there's hope at the end
as we walk through the valley hand in hand.

Even though I walk through the valley of the shadow of death,
I will fear no evil, for you are with me;
your rod and your staff, they comfort me.
Psalm 23:4

TREE OF LIFE

The tree of life stood all alone
in the Garden that dark day,
calling out to Adam and Eve
to stop along the way.

To test the fruit that God had made
and then forbid to take.
He surely didn't mean "Don't touch,"
its fruit to just forsake.

Eating it gave knowledge
of good and evil done.
What harm could be in eating
while it ripened in the sun?

Another "Tree of Life" stood
alone upon a hill.
It too calls out to all mankind
and continues even still.

To partake what this tree offers,
the salvation that is brought
to every soul that seeks out
the gift that Christ has bought.

By hanging upon this rugged tree,
Christ died there for us all.
Do not walk past this Tree of Life,
but listen to its call.

God calls for us to touch this tree,
this tree that eases strife.
We have two trees to choose from,
choose Christ's blessed "Tree of Life".

*"Blessed are those who wash their robes, that they may have the right
to the tree of life and may go through the gates into the city."*
Revelation 22:14

TRUE CHRISTIANITY

Do you think you're righteous when you take a Christian stand?
Perhaps you think you're better when, in praise, you raise your hand.
Do you think you're greater when surveying those around
while looking at their behaviors, they've been judged and "guilty" found?

Do you think you know more from all the books that you have read?
Blessed because of money given and the many prayers you've said?
Do you feel that, as a Christian, you stand high above the rest?
On the scale of good behavior, you have surely passed the test?

Do you point out others failures like you've never had your own,
when, if all was revealed and open, your own failures would be shown?
In your efforts to be a Christian, are you judgmental, arrogant, mean?
In your exclusive self-righteous manner, is the "heart" of Jesus seen?

Rather strive for deep compassion, see beyond all life's despair,
view others as God intended, don't go judging and compare.
Let the heart and light of Jesus shine through all the things you do,
leading others to the Father, transforming countless lives anew.

*"Be careful not to do your 'acts of righteousness' before men, to be seen by them.
If you do, you will have no reward from your Father in heaven."*
Matthew 6:1

UNCONDITIONAL LOVE

When I feel the wind against my face, I can feel God's gentle touch;
He lets me know He's by my side and loves me very much.

The wind may be soft and soothing, or briskly rustling through the trees,
and surely all of nature feels God's love within that breeze.

I may not understand such love, a love I don't deserve.
The love that He bestows on me He gives without reserve.

I may fail in my daily walk, even failing those I love.
To them I may never be good enough, nor measure up to God above.

But I know in all my failings, God's love is always here.
I can feel Him in my surroundings and, like nature, know He's near.

For when I feel that gentle breeze, wafting cool against my tears,
I know I have all I'll ever need throughout my days and years.

He gives me unconditional love, and He gives the same to you.
We can feel God's touch in the gentle breeze, a love that's real and true.

This is love: not that we love God, but that he loved us
and sent his Son as an atoning sacrifice for our sins.
1 John 4:10

WALKING BLIND

I was blind. I could not see.
But it wasn't my "eyes" that failed me.
It was lack of faith and hope and love;
not "seeing" the grace from God above.

I searched for answers as though I was blind,
feeling my way as I sought to find
what I most needed, reaching out,
knowing, though sightless, I never should doubt.

For God was there with me, holding my hand,
lifting me up when I could not stand.
Leading the way in my world of dark;
lighting my path that was lonely and stark.

I'd chosen that darkness, I know it is true,
and only my faith has helped see me through.
For faith can restore sight, when on bended knee,
I surely was blind, but now I can see.

It just took some faith and the power of belief
to heal my "blindness" and bring me relief
from the darkness that surrounded my spirit and soul.
Now I have "sight" wherever I go.

He replied, "Whether he is a sinner or not, I don't know.
One thing I do know, I was blind but now I see!"
John 9:25

WE ARE HEARD

When it's dark and quiet, and we're hurting inside,
and we're pouring out our soul to the Lord,
please know there's a mighty God up above
that listens and hears every word.

When life disappoints and nothing goes right,
and we're tired of this "dog-eat-dog" world,
God hears our pain through our soul-wrenching prayers,
and His unbounded love is unfurled.

When a loved one has died and we feel all alone,
and our grief is more than we can bear,
God knows of our loss and He feels our deep pain,
His comfort and compassion He will share.

And when good things happen in this world we live in,
and we thank God for His blessings from above,
we can know that God hears our rejoicing and praise,
for He's a God of celebration and love.

So never stop praying and talking to God,
for He truly wants to hear every word.
Don't doubt that God hears every prayer that we pray,
for He assures us that each one is heard!

... but God has surely listened and heard my voice in prayer.
Praise be to God, who has not rejected my prayer
or withheld his love from me!
Psalm 66:19-20

WE DON'T ALWAYS KNOW

We don't always know others' heartaches;
don't know how their life has been.
We don't know what happens behind closed doors
though we may be their closest friend.

We don't always know what they're going through;
may not know their deepest pain.
We don't see the tears they shed at night,
nor daytime efforts to restrain.

We may not know their loss of loved ones,
nor see health issues that abound;
don't see their financial burdens
or the marriage that broke down.

We don't really know all is well with them
when they tell us all is good.
We don't know if they are happy
and all is going as it should.

But often that is just the case,
we don't see what's really there.
They lend their smiles, we hear them laugh,
but their burdens they do not share.

They do not talk about the pain
behind the wall that's put in place.
Not wanting others to see the hurt
behind the smile upon their face.

But this we can be sure of
when we take the time to pray,
God will walk right there beside them
when they feel life's gone astray.

We do not know God's plan for them,
nor the path that they must take,
but we know He will be there for them
with a love He won't forsake.

... because God has said, "Never will I leave you; never will I forsake you."
Hebrews 13:5

WHAT DO YOU HEAR

What do you hear when the Word is preached
when you sit in the church's pew,
as the pastor preaches right from wrong,
and what we should and shouldn't do?

What do you hear when the choir sings
"Hallelujahs" to the Lord?
Do you feel that you're unworthy
for all the good that you've ignored?

What do you hear when it's still and silent?
Are voices crying out in your head,
shouting recriminations
for bad things you've done and said?

What do you hear when Christ is calling
from the pages of the Living Word?
Do you hear of His love and mercy and grace?
Is His voice truly sought and heard?

What do you hear when you say you are worthy
because of the many "good works" you have done?
Scripture tells us we are not saved by our actions,
but rather through the death of God's Son.

What do you hear when Christ is crying,
"Father, forgive them for the wrongs that they do.
Let, then, My sacrifice be their salvation,
so that they hear what is righteous and true!"

*All of us have become like one who is unclean,
and all our righteous acts are like filthy rags...*
Isaiah 64:6

Jesus said, "Father, forgive them, for they do not know what they are doing."
Luke 23:34

WHAT REALLY WOULD HAVE JESUS DONE

What really would have Jesus done
with the homeless on the street?
Would He have bought them a nice hot meal and shoes for their weary feet?

What really would have Jesus done
with cries from a hurting soul?
Would He have dried their falling tears and stopped their steady flow?

What really would have Jesus done
for the blind man seeking sight?
Would He have touched those blinded eyes and made the darkness light?

What really would have Jesus done
for the cripple who could not walk
or for the mute who wanted more than anything to talk?

What really would have Jesus done
for those who believed in Him?
Would He have touched them with His love and forgave them of their sin?

We know what Jesus would have done.
It's all written in God's Word.
He has given us direction and His path is most assured.

So, when you ask "What would Jesus do?"
when confronted with decisions to make,
you'll really know what you must do and what action you must take.

If you ever are uncertain,
you'll know right where to look,
you'll know He's given us guidance, and it's found in God's Holy Book.

And whatever you do, whether in word or deed,
do it all in the name of the Lord Jesus,
giving thanks to God the Father through him.
Colossians 3:17

WHEELS IN MOTION

Thank you, Lord, for your body and blood
which you shed upon the cross.
A wonderful gift which you freely gave
and certainly Earth's greatest loss.

Your death was necessary to save our souls;
there could be no other way.
You willingly walked the hill to the cross,
knowing death was the plan that day.

It wasn't pretty as you trudged the hill;
you'd already been beaten and flayed.
You needed help with the heavy cross,
knowing the price that must be paid.

When we think back through your life, Lord,
and the significance of your birth,
that event set the wheels in motion
of God's life, as man, on Earth.

But, oh, the sorrow that would follow
when the disciples learned of your fate.
To live your life with one goal in mind.
Your deepest love to demonstrate.

Thank you for your birth, Lord,
for your life and for your death.
Thank you for your forgiveness
before taking your final breath.

Thanks for your love in coming to Earth,
born to die for humanity.
Help us daily to remember that sacrifice
and how you lovingly set us free!

"Do not let your hearts be troubled. Trust in God; trust also in me.
In my Father's house are many rooms; if it were not so,
I would have told you. I am going there to prepare a place for you.
And if I go and prepare a place for you, I will come back and take you to be with me
that you also may be where I am. You know the way to the place where I am going."
John 14:1-4

WHEN GOD COMES KNOCKING

When God comes knocking at your door,
are you listening from within?
Are you receptive to His call?
Are you prepared to let Him in?

When God comes knocking at your door,
is your house all tidy and neat,
or is it cluttered with worldly goods;
a stumbling block to your feet?

When God comes knocking at your door
have you prepared a place
to welcome Him in to rest awhile,
a haven from life's hectic pace?

When God comes knocking at your door
are you dressed and ready to go?
When He says to you, "Come follow Me,"
will you leave behind all and do so?

You must be prepared for that special knock
when God has chosen your door.
Be at the threshold, waiting for Him,
to answer His knock and more.

"Here I am! I stand at the door and knock.
If anyone hears my voice and opens the door,
I will come in and eat with him, and he with me."
Revelation 3:20

WHEN LIFE GETS IN THE WAY

We try, dear Lord, to do your will.
We strive to do what's right.
But life just seems to get in the way
though we try with all our might.
We cannot live life on our own.
We must always depend on you.
And not let life get in the way
of all we say and do.
Help us to walk the narrow path,
we know it's walked by few.
Please take our hand and guide our steps
as we keep our eyes on you.
Help us not to drag our feet,
looking around us in despair,
or cry and moan when our path gets steep,
blaming you when life's not fair.
Help us to keep a sweet disposition,
placing a smile upon our face;
not letting trials, sorrows, worries,
slow our ever-steady pace.
Help us to be slow to anger.
Remind us to lend a cheerful hand.
And when life tries to push us down,
help us, Lord, to take a stand.
Help us always make the right decisions,
knowing we can depend on you each day;
always striving to do the right thing
when life gets in the way!

Do what is right and good in the Lord's sight,
so that it may go well with you ...
Deuteronomy 6:18

WHEN OUR HEARTS ARE HEAVY

When our hearts are feeling heavy, Lord,
we know that you are near.
Feeling the weight of life's many burdens,
there is nothing we should fear.

Sometimes life takes a sudden turn
though we may often question why;
not knowing the rhyme or reason,
nor comprehending, though we try.

We know not what the future holds,
but we place all in your hands,
and no matter what may come our way,
we know we're in your plans.

Help us, Lord, to be stronger
in the trials of each day,
and remember you are with us
no matter what may come our way.

*"And surely I will be with you always,
to the very end of the age."*
Matthew 28:20

WHEN THE HAMMER HITS THE NAIL

The job's not started, the deed's not done,
until the hammer hits the nail.
Life will always be this way.
We must move forward without fail.

In moving forward in this life
we must take the hammer in our hand
and start the job that must begin
to finish what God has planned.

And once the nail is driven through
and you know the job's begun,
you can pull out the nail but the hole's still there,
you can't take back what's been done.

Jesus came with a plan and a purpose
to hang on the cross-fashioned tree.
It all started when the hammer hit the nail
in His sacrifice for you and me.

Though this scene seems both stark and cold,
it was an event that had to take place.
For Christ came to Earth for this purpose,
to save the human race.

So, thank you, God, for the hammer,
and thank you, too, for the nail.
Thankful Jesus was willing to accept these tools
and to die on the cross without fail.

And, yes, the nail has been removed,
and the hole and scar are still there.
A reminder when the hammer hit the nail
and of His loving sacrifice so rare!

*This man was handed over to you by God's set purpose and
foreknowledge; and you, with the help of wicked men,
put him to death by nailing him to the cross.*
Acts 2:23

WHEN YOUR SPIRIT'S BEING CHALLENGED

When your Spirit's being challenged
    by the evil of the day,
look to Jesus, the Lord and Savior,
    get on your knees and pray.

Evil words and thoughts and stories
    assault the senses at every turn.
Be prepared for this daily battle,
    wear God's armor strong and firm.

Steer clear of the murky waters
    that can flood the mind and soul,
muddied by this day's free living,
    lack of morals and self-control.

Remember to think only good thoughts,
    read the Bible to tide you through,
during waves of doubt and worry,
    think of Scripture, tried and true.

For when the day has ended,
    and you ponder the day just spent,
think not of hurts and gossip,
    angry words and sad dissent.

Christ is walking on the waters
    through the turbulence of your mind.
He is reaching out to save you,
    abundant peace and calm you'll find.

When your Spirit's being challenged
    by the evil of the day,
remember the Lord and Savior,
    remember to kneel and pray.

When the disciples saw him walking on the lake, they were terrified.
"It's a ghost," they said, and cried out in fear.
But Jesus immediately said to them: "Take courage! It is I. Don't be afraid."
Matthew 14:26-27

WHERE ANGELS GATHER

The angels gather 'round about
when we sing songs to the Lord.
They gleefully join in the chorus,
harmonizing with every chord.

The angels gather 'round about
as we bow our head each day
and praise the Heavenly Father
each and every time we pray.

The angels gather 'round about
catching teardrops falling down,
and turn them into diamonds
to be placed in Heaven's crown.

The angels gather 'round about
at the birth of every child,
remembering the greatest birth of all,
of Him both meek and mild.

The angels gather 'round about
for every sinner that is saved;
rejoicing in celebration
for the price our Savior paid.

The angels gather 'round about
at the death of every saint,
knowing they will soon see Jesus
as they enter Heaven's gate.

The angels gather 'round about
before the Heavenly throne,
lifting praises to the Father
for the deep love He has shown.

For he will command His angels concerning you
to guard you in all your ways...
Psalm 91:11

WHERE IS YOUR LADDER LEANING

What wall is your ladder leaning against
when climbing through life each day?
Upon which height are you trying to reach
when seeking to find your way?

Are you trying to reach a bundle of wealth
as you're searching for that "pie in the sky,"
or trying to grasp all that life gives
and coming up empty and dry?

Are you trying to take hold of the things in this world
that really have no meaning at all
as you climb the ascent with unease as you grope;
fearfully trembling through life that you'll fall?

Perhaps half way up you've realized
that your ladder is in the wrong place,
and you have to back down and start over again
while seeking God's wisdom and grace.

Choose wisely the wall upon which you lean
the ladder you're starting to climb,
and know that He's with you each "rung" of the way,
and the top is in God's perfect-planned time.

Trust in the Lord with all your heart
and lean not on your own understanding ...
Proverbs 3:5

WHICH LASH DID JESUS TAKE FOR ME

Which lash did Jesus take for me?
Which welt across His back
did He take on for all my sin
and for all the good I lack?

Which thorn that stabbed His tender brow
did He take on for me?
It pierced the skin and blood ran down,
but it was I that He could see.

Which nail in His hands and feet
were hammered for my sin?
He was willing to be nailed to the cross
allowing salvation to enter in.

Which taunt did Jesus listen to
when they threw lots for His robe?
Knowing He'd never need it again,
for He was leaving this earthly globe.

Which thought was on the soldier's mind
when he pierced the Savior's side?
Jesus' pain was more than man should bear,
and His sorrow He could not hide.

Which decision are you going to make?
You know what you must do.
The decision should be to follow Christ
in light of the suffering He endured for you.

He himself bore our sins in his body on the tree,
so that we might die to sins and live for righteousness;
by his wounds you have been healed.
1 Peter 2:24

WHILE NO ONE IS WATCHING

While no one is watching, the thief takes from the shelf
what he hopes will never be missed.
He prays for a job and a place he can rest, release from a life full of risk.

While no one is watching, the clown enters in;
the circus is about to begin.
Though a smile is painted on a face that is sad,
they can't see past his fake comic grin.

While no one is watching, she gives all she has.
Some loose change is all she can spare.
But it truly is more than she'll ever really know,
she'll be blessed for what she could share.

While no one is watching, a tear trickles down;
though unseen is quickly wiped away.
But time surely heals a heart that's been broken,
God lovingly planned it that way.

While no one is watching, do you think it's okay
to cuss, yell, and angrily swear?
Do you gossip and talk about those who you know,
thinking it's okay since they are not there?

While no one is watching, as we look in the mirror,
are we looking at who others see?
Is there faith and compassion and trust in our face,
is our reflection what we want it to be?

While no one is watching, always strive for the best,
with the knowledge of all we'll achieve.
We can then always know that the person gazing
back is the one in who we can believe.

While no one is watching, God surely does see
every deed, every prayer, every plea,
every sorrow, every hurt, every regret and rejection,
every pain that others can't see.

While no one is watching, we fall to our knees,
praying for forgiveness of sin.
The Heavenly Father sees us as we're kneeling,
where surely grace and mercy begin.

*"But when you give to the needy, do not let your left hand know
what your right hand is doing, so that your giving may be in secret.
Then your Father, who sees what is done in secret, will reward you."*
Matthew 6:3-4

WHO IS THIS MAN CALLED JESUS

Who is this man called Jesus, who came to Earth as man
to live and die for each of us
with a purpose and a plan.

Who is this man called Teacher, who as a youth did know
He had wisdom for the scholars;
in His teachings it did show.

Who is this man called Jehovah, calling fisherman to His side,
inviting them to follow Him;
their needs He would provide.

Who is this man called Immanuel, who turned water into wine;
who miraculously fed the thousands
and with sinners He did dine.

Who is this man called Prince of Peace, revealing how to live and pray.
He portrayed true love in action
with compassion on display.

Who is this man called Redeemer, who came to Earth to die,
to hang upon the wooden cross,
sacrificed for you and I.

Who is this man called Messiah, Lord of lords and King of kings,
Wonderful Counselor, Blessed Savior.
Salvation is what He brings.

Yes, this man who is called Jesus, awaits for us at Heaven's throne.
No greater Friend and Savior;
no greater love ever shown!

And he will be called Wonderful Counselor, Mighty God,
Everlasting Father, Prince of Peace.
Isaiah 9:6

WHO KNEW?

Who makes the beautiful, white, heavenly snow
and makes the mighty wind-driven gusts blow?
Who makes the refreshing soft-falling rain
that quickly flows down the window's glass pane?
Who makes the beautiful, colorful, flowers
blooming in the season's spring, warm, sun-kissed showers?
And who tosses the waves of the wide-open sea,
and in its mad rush, would be called tsunami?

Who gave warmth to the mighty sun's, brilliant, bright light
and gave the moon's glow in the twilight of night?
Who gave us the tears that down our face flow,
and gave us emotions and feelings that show?
Who gave us love when love can seem lost
and truly did demonstrate how much love can cost?
Who made the universe, the planets, the stars,
and decided we'd live on the Earth and not Mars?

Who knew us long before our arrival to Earth,
and knew and scheduled the day of our birth?
Who knew God would come to Earth as a man,
with a purpose in mind and a salvation plan?
Who knew of our sin and the complexities of life,
and knew of our worries and stresses and strife?
Who can give us peace and rest to our souls;
direct our path and know where our path goes?

We know it is God, our Father and Friend,
who will teach us and guide us, whom we can depend.
Know that His covenants are sanctioned and planned,
and are promises, through life, upon which we can stand.
Who knew that creation would bring us this far,
which all started in Genesis and the birth of Earth's star?
Look not at the past, but where our future will be,
when we meet at God's throne and the glory we'll see!

In the beginning God created the heavens and the earth.
Genesis 1:1

WHO PACKS YOUR PARACHUTE?

Do you put your life and trust
in another person's hands,
having faith that you'll be safe, no matter where life lands?

Do you believe your parachute
is packed with loving care,
knowing that when it's needed, it will open up with flare?

Is your parachute a phone call
when you're feeling all alone?
Perhaps a hug when needed and a friend's love clearly shown?

Is it a hand to help you
when feeling pressures of the day,
or perhaps a voice to guide you when you feel you've lost your way?

It may be a total stranger,
someone you truly do not know,
or a personal friend who's there for you no matter where you go.

Perhaps God's love and mercy
is the parachute you need.
His grace is right there for you, with life's burdens finally freed.

And when that parachute opens
and you've drifted to the ground,
do you thank the Lord Almighty that you landed safe and sound?

Please know that there is inner peace
knowing someone cares enough
to safely pack your parachute for when storms of life get rough.

Yes, thank God for those parachutes,
packed for you with loving care,
that will open when most needed when you whisper fervent prayer!

Now faith is being sure of what we hope for and certain of what we do not see.
Hebrews 11:1

WHY JESUS CAME TO EARTH

When the world seems troubled, and you question life's worth,
and you ponder Christ's mission in coming to Earth,
please know His trip was highly ordained
and it happened just as the prophets proclaimed.
He came as a babe on the near edge of night
with angels rejoicing in Heavenly light.
He grew up working as a carpenter's son,
winning the hearts of most everyone.
They could plainly see when He became a man
that He was sent by God with a mission and plan.
His purpose was to seek the lonely and lost,
and, being God's Son, He knew the cost.
His goal coming to Earth was the cross on the hill;
God's plan of salvation He came to fulfill.
So, when you're feeling lost at the end of the day,
remember Christ came to show us the way.
And when this life's done, and you've left this Earth,
you'll understand Christ's mission and what it was worth!

*But the angel said to them, "Do not be afraid. I bring you good news of great joy
that will be for all the people. Today in the town of David a Savior has been
born to you; he is Christ the Lord.*
Luke 2:10-11

WINNING

"You can't win if you don't play,"
is what the gambler said.
Perhaps that's how those dueling felt,
risking fate of death instead.

The millionaire felt he played and won
the best game of his life,
but he lost much more than he bargained for,
losing family, friends, and wife.

In business, many strive to win
as they scurry for first place;
grasping and clawing to the top,
seeking first in life's rat race.

Greed and wealth may drive us
onward, upward, in our climb.
It can also be detrimental
in the counting of every dime.

In our efforts to be the very best,
always striving to get ahead,
perhaps taking the focus off ourselves
is the better path instead.

With Jesus, no need to out perform
to gain the greatest prize.
No need to strive to be the best
to be a winner in His eyes.

With Christ, you can win if you don't play,
because you'll always win with Him.
You just need to believe He died for you.
You "won" when He died for sin.

But thanks be to God!
He gives us the victory through our Lord Jesus Christ.
1 Corinthians 15:57

WITHOUT JESUS

Without Jesus, there would have been no virgin birth
by Mary, sweet and dear;
there would have been no Christmas manger;
no wise men drawing near.

Without Jesus, there would have been no miracle
of Lazarus from the tomb;
no feeding of the thousands;
no John from Elizabeth's womb.

Without Jesus, they would have been just fishermen,
Andrew, Peter, James and John;
no purpose in their mission;
no Gospel to pass on.

Matthew would have stayed a tax collector;
Saul, a legalistic Pharisee;
no turning water into wine;
no walking on the sea.

Without Jesus, there would be no Good Fridays;
no early Easter morns;
no worshiping on Sundays;
no cross or crown of thorns.

Without Jesus, there would be no life after death;
there would be no blessed hope;
no comfort from the grief of loss;
no Savior to help us cope.

Let's be thankful there is Jesus,
who came to live as man;
who was willing to come and live and die,
to fulfill God's mighty plan.

Yes, we can celebrate Easter mornings;
break the bread and share the wine;
be baptized in the Spirit;
gain salvation, love divine!

"I am the good shepherd; I know my sheep and my sheep know me - just as the
Father knows me and I know the Father - and I lay down my life for the sheep."
John 10:14-15

WORDS OF WISDOM

Feed your faith, starve your fears.
Laugh don't cry, dry your tears.

Speak the truth, talk the walk.
On your journey, walk that talk.

Life is busy, keep the pace.
Run to win, win the race.

Know you're human, you will sin.
When you fail, try again.

Pray to God, face to face.
Know Christ Jesus, saving grace.

Reaching out, take a hand.
Touch a heart, serve fellow man.

Search for needs, show you care.
On your knees, say a prayer.

Hunger calls, feed the poor.
Help the weak, heal the sore.

Be a servant, gain the prize.
Reward is found, in paradise.

Renew your strength, mount up with wings.
Wait on the Lord, King of kings.

On the cross, Christ did die.
When feeling lost, on Him rely.

Preach the Gospel, share God's Word.
Lift your voice, you will be heard.

Believe in Jesus, salvation found.
At Heaven's gate, you will be crowned.

When you die, this life will end.
Christ will say, "Well done, My friend!"

Blessed is the man who finds wisdom,
the man who gains understanding ...
Proverbs 3:13

WORDS TO THE DISCIPLES

"You have seen Me, yet still not believe?
Why really must this be so?
I am right here in flesh and blood,
and My mission you do know."

"I've come to show you each the way
as we travel through this life.
It matters not what may arise
through trials and daily strife."

"For I've shown you all that you must do;
the path that you must walk.
I've shown you how to love and serve,
how to live and walk the talk."

"I hope that I've instilled in you
the desire to do your best
and know that all your efforts
will be sanctified and blessed."

"As I leave now for the Father,
I give you each My love,
and look forward to seeing you again
when we meet at God's throne above!"

*On the evening of that first day of the week,
when the disciples were together, with the doors locked
for fear of the Jews, Jesus came and stood among them and said,
"Peace be with you!" After he said this, he showed them his hands and side.
The disciples were overjoyed when they saw the Lord.
Again, Jesus said, "Peace be with you! As the Father has sent me, I am sending you."
And with that he breathed on them and said,
"Receive the Holy Spirit."*
John 20:19-22

WORK, LOVE, DANCE, SING, AND LIVE

Work like you don't need the money.
Enjoy the work that you do.
Put your all into what you are doing,
and life's treasures will be there for you!

Love like nobody has hurt you.
You can, you know, if you try.
And if hurts build up around you,
love anyway, though you may cry.

Dance like nobody is watching.
Dance and twirl with all of your might.
Rejoice in the life you've been given.
Feel like dancing both day and night.

Sing like nobody is listening.
It matters not if you're singing off key.
The fact is, your soul is rejoicing;
an example of how we should be.

Live as if Earth is paradise.
In doing so, you'll be the one
that when this life is over,
God will greet you and say "well done!"

"His master replied, 'Well done, good and faithful servant!
You have been faithful with a few things;
I will put you in charge of many things.
Come and share your master's happiness!'".
Matthew 25:23

WRITTEN ON YOUR HEARTS

There's a letter written on our hearts;
it's written by Christ above.
It's known and read by many, and it's written there with love.

It's not written there with man-made ink,
nor chiseled or engraved on stone.
It's written there with the Spirit of the Living God alone.

Unlike the Ten Commandments
written by God's mighty hand,
engraved upon the mountain rock and carried down to man.

The Commandments came with glory,
engraved tablets shared with all.
They were given for strict adherence, and, to man, a wake-up call.

They came to Moses with glory,
glory fading though it was.
Would not this letter now written bring more glory in all it does?

For Christ removed the old covenant;
He has taken the veil away.
Through this "letter" written on our hearts, He says what He must say.

And now with unveiled faces
reflecting His glory there,
being transformed in His likeness, His letter we must share.

*Now if the ministry that brought death, which was engraved in letters on stone,
came with glory, so that the Israelites could not look steadily at the face
of Moses because of its glory, fading though it was,
will not the ministry of the Spirit be even more glorious?*
2 Corinthians 3:7-8

YOUR AMAZING GRACE

I looked up at the stars one night,
your glory I could see,
and wondered, while just sitting there,
why you lived and died for me?

I'm just a speck among billions
that live upon this Earth.
The sacrifice you have made for us
is priceless in its worth.

We would have lived a life without
a purpose or a plan
if you had not been willing
to come to Earth as man.

You know our every temptation,
our loves, our guilts, our fears.
You know the joy in our laughter
and the sorrow in our tears.

You know our every struggle
as we push to get ahead.
You know our every striving
to follow the life you led.

Yes, I look up at the starry sky,
and your glory I see there.
I thank you for your amazing grace,
so beautiful and rare!

*May the grace of the Lord Jesus Christ, and the love of God,
and the fellowship of the Holy Spirit be with you all.*
2 Corinthians 13:14

YOUR PLANS

What if God has other plans from the ones you've planned yourself?
Do you think perhaps it would be wise
to ask God for His help?

Take a moment to just step back from all the things you've planned,
seeking God's directions
as you gently take His hand.

Allowing Him to guide and lead, sharing all that you must do,
and trust Him in His guidance
on the path that's walked by few.

He knows the trials and hardships you will encounter on your way.
He knows the troubles and burdens
that you'll come across each day.

You must embrace all He provides on this earthly walk you take,
knowing He's right there for you
through each "wrong turn" and mistake.

He always knows what's best for you as He grants both mercy and grace.
You'll thank Him one day for His guidance
when you see Him face to face!

"For I know the plans I have for you," declares the Lord,
"plans to prosper you and not to harm you,
plans to give you hope and a future."
Jeremiah 29:11

Printed in the United States
By Bookmasters